Mindset of Permanent Weight Loss

Mindset of Permanent Weight Loss

Yvette Hewett

Table of Contents

Mindset for Permanent Weight Loss

BY YVETTE HEWETT

Successful People	Unsuccessful People
Self-Improvement Focused	Weight-Loss Focused
Progress-Focused	Limitations-Focused
Behavior-Focused	Food-Focused
Self-Compassion	Self-Criticism
Long-Term Goals	Quick Fixes
Setbacks are Learning Opportunities	Setbacks are a Reason to Quit
Planned Meals and Snacks	Impulsive Decision-Making
Prepare Healthy Options	Rely on Convenience Food
Healthy Alternatives	Lack of Preparation
Rely on Removing Cravings	Relying on Willpower
Consistent	Quit and Start Over All the Time
Regular Balanced Meals	Skipping Meals
Mindful Eating	Mindless Snacking
Mentor Support	Lack of Support
Track Yourself	Avoid Self-Monitoring
Prioritize Adequate Sleep	Poor Sleep Hygiene
Celebrate Non-Scale Victories	Fixating on the Scale
Focusing on Intrinsic Rewards	Relying on Food Rewards
Focusing on Health and Energy	Focusing on the Scale Only
Viewing Setbacks as Temporary	Giving Up Easily
Adjust Strategies when Needed	Lack of Resilience
Taking Accountability	Using Excuses

Unpacking the Mindsets That Make or Break Your Goals

Weight loss may be a desired outcome of self-improvement, but it should not be the sole purpose. By prioritizing overall health, cultivating positive habits, and celebrating all forms of progress, we can embark on an adventure of sustainable transformation extending far beyond the numbers on the scale.

Psychology plays a crucial and often underestimated role in achieving permanent weight loss. While food choices and nutritional intake are important, permanent success hinges on more than just what you eat on your plate.

Forget fad diets and quick fixes. The real key to achieving and maintaining weight loss lies within your mind. While food choices matter, permanent success relies on the often-ignored power of psychology. It is the silent driver influencing your motivation, habits, and emotional responses, ultimately determining whether you reach your goals or stumble along the way.

A positive, empowered mindset propels you forward, navigating challenges with resilience. Conversely, a negative or self-doubting mindset acts like a brake, hindering progress and fueling frustration.

This is not an exhaustive list, but by reflecting on these behaviors, you can identify your personal "passengers." Are there sabotaging passengers hitching a ride, holding you back? Perhaps the inner critic berates you after a slip-up, or the autopilot steers you toward unhealthy choices. Alternatively, are you fostering supportive passengers, like the compassionate coach or the mindful eater?

Remember, permanent weight loss is not about conforming to a rigid list. It is about understanding your unique mental landscape and empowering yourself. Once you identify your sabotaging passengers, you can gently encourage them to disembark and invite supportive ones aboard. By tuning your mind, you will find the motivation, resilience, and self-awareness to navigate your weight loss adventure with confidence and achieve permanent success.

Start your introspection today. Unlock the power of your mind, and watch your weight loss adventure transform from a bumpy ride to a smooth, empowered path toward a healthier you.

Chapter 1
Weight-Loss Focused vs. Self-Improvement Focused

Weight-Loss Focused

In the quest for a healthier, happier you, weight loss often takes center stage. However, solely focusing on the scale's numbers, while seemingly straightforward, is a psychological trap, hindering your chances of permanent success.

The weight loss mindset narrows your vision, turning the scale into the primary judge of progress. This overlooks an abundance of other facets of health and well-being, like energy levels, mood, sleep quality, and improved body composition.

When weight loss becomes the main focus, you disconnect from your body's natural hunger and satiety signals. This leads to ignoring your intuitive cues, overeating or under eating, and ultimately, hindering progress.

Fixating on weight loss risks neglecting other crucial aspects of well-being, like social connections, emotional management, and physical activity enjoyment. This creates an unsustainable approach prioritizing a number over holistic well-being.

Obsessing over weight loss prioritizes immediate wins over long-term progress. You might select quick fixes or restrictive diets for rapid weight loss, neglecting sustainable habit formation and healthy lifestyle changes.

Weight loss is a dynamic process, with plateaus and occasional setbacks, and focusing solely on the scale amplifies these challenges, leading to discouragement and frustration when progress slows down.

This wears down motivation and makes long-term commitment difficult.

When self-worth is tied to the ever-fluctuating numbers on the scale, setbacks trigger feelings of failure and loss of control. This decreases self-confidence and reduces the belief in one's own ability to achieve permanent changes. It also creates a fear of food, leading to restrictive diets and unhealthy relationships with food. This fosters anxiety, guilt, and a negative cycle of yo-yo dieting.

When solely focused on weight loss, healthy food becomes a chore or even a form of punishment. This brews feelings of dread and negativity toward healthy eating, undermining its long-term sustainability and enjoyment.

This weight loss obsession shifts your focus from appreciating your body's capabilities and resilience to fixating on perceived flaws, which leads to a negative self-image, and ultimately, hinders progress.

Primarily focusing on weight loss offers a seductive, yet limiting, path to success. It narrows your vision, limits motivation, and promotes unhealthy relationships with food and exercise.

Self-Improvement Focused

Framing weight loss as self-improvement, rather than just weight loss, unlocks a powerful psychological advantage. This shift in mindset fosters motivation, resilience, and sustainable behavioral change, ultimately increasing your chances of achieving and maintaining healthy habits.

Viewing weight loss as self-improvement moves the focus from the goal of reaching a specific number on the scale to the ongoing process of building healthier habits, learning new skills, and strengthening your personal well-being. This intrinsic motivation is more sustainable and resilient than extrinsic motivators, like fitting into clothes or societal expectations.

It allows you to connect to your deeper values, such as health, resilience, and self-respect. This creates a sense of purpose and meaning going beyond momentary desires and fueling long-term commitment.

When focused on self-improvement, every step counts. You celebrate increased energy levels, improved sleep, and the development of new healthy habits, not just the numbers on the scale. This keeps you motivated, even when progress seems slow or there is no drop on the scale, fostering a positive feedback loop.

A self-improvement focus encourages a growth mindset. Setbacks become opportunities to learn and adapt, not failures. You focus on analyzing your choices, refining your strategies, and building resilience toward future challenges.

You invest in learning healthy coping mechanisms to manage stress, cravings, and emotional triggers. This equips you with the tools to navigate challenges without resorting to unhealthy habits.

Self-improvement involves consistent effort and discipline. With each healthy choice you make, you build your self-control and willpower, making it easier to navigate temptations and stay on track in the long run.

It shifts the focus from restrictive diets and quick fixes to acquiring and integrating healthy habits into your daily life. You learn to cook nutritious meals, move your body, and prioritize sleep and stress management. These skills empower you to make sustainable changes without relying on external control.

Self-improvement emphasizes finding what works best for you. You experiment with different approaches, tailor your routines to your lifestyle, and embrace flexibility. This fosters a sustainable and less boring process personalized to your unique needs and preferences.

Viewing weight loss as self-improvement helps you see it as a lifelong adventure, not a quick fix. This promotes a focus on long-term well-being and a commitment to continuous growth and evolution, preventing discouragement and promoting permanent change.

Framing weight loss as self-improvement is a powerful psychological tool sparking intrinsic motivation, building resilience, and encouraging sustainable habit formation. By viewing the process as a journey of personal growth, you cultivate a deeper connection to your health, celebrate non-scale victories, and build a foundation for permanent change beyond the numbers on the scale. Weight loss is about becoming a better version of yourself, not just reaching a specific number. Embrace the process, learn, grow, and celebrate every step on your path to a healthier, happier you.

The decision to move from a weight-loss-centric mindset to a self-improvement approach is a powerful one. It is a commitment to nurturing our well-being, honoring our bodies, and building a healthy relationship with food and movement. This shift requires self-awareness, a willingness to learn, and a commitment to unlearning harmful patterns.

Chapter 2
Limitations-Focused vs. Progress-Focused

Limitations-Focused

In the battle of the bulge, the weapons we choose can tip the scales in our favor. Two of the most potent tools in our arsenal are focus and perspective. But where do we aim them: at the tiny morsels of progress or the seemingly insurmountable obstacles between us and our goals?

Limitations-focused individuals are often bogged down by the mental quicksand of self-doubt by magnifying hurdles, fixating on restrictions, and dwelling on what they "cannott" have. Acknowledging your limitations is an essential step. However, fixating on food and ability constraints, while seemingly realistic, is a psychological trap, diminishing your chances of achieving permanent weight loss.

When you dwell on what you "cannot" eat or what you "cannot" do, you reinforce those limitations in your mind. This leads to a self-fulfilling prophecy, where you start avoiding certain foods or activities, hindering your potential for positive change.

Fixating on limitations narrows your vision, overlooking your existing strengths and potential for improvement. You ignore opportunities to explore new healthy foods, discover different forms of movement, and build on your existing abilities.

Focusing on limitations highlights perceived weaknesses, like genetics, time constraints, or lack of knowledge. This reduces belief in your own ability to make positive changes and achieve your goals, undermining motivation and effort.

Constant focus on limitations breeds discouragement and apathy. You might feel overwhelmed by the perceived difficulty of the process, leading to decreased motivation and a tendency to abandon your goals altogether.

Dwelling on food and ability limitations leads to a victim mentality. You attribute your difficulties to external factors or inherent constraints, diminishing your sense of balance and control over your health and well-being.

When you fixate on limitations, you might blame food producers, genetics, or even your environment for your struggles. This externalization of responsibility prevents you from taking ownership of your choices and hinders your ability to make the necessary changes.

Focusing on limitations erodes your belief in your ability to succeed. You start doubting your willpower, perseverance, and capacity for change, leading to a defeatist attitude and decreased effort.

Fixating on limitations creates a fear of venturing outside your comfort zone. You are less likely to experiment with new recipes, try different workouts, or challenge yourself to improve your physical capabilities.

When you solely focus on what you cannot do, you miss out on valuable opportunities for personal discovery. You might have hidden talents or untapped potential in regard to healthy cooking, physical activity, or other aspects of well-being.

Focusing on limitations traps you in negative stereotypes about yourself or your body type. You might believe "I am just built this way" or "thin people just have faster metabolisms," creating self-fulfilling prophecies restricting your potential.

When you fixate on limitations, you become hesitant to try new things or expand your comfort zone. This hinders your ability to discover new activities, healthy recipes, or exercise routines that could be truly beneficial for your weight loss adventure.

Focusing on limitations provides justification for inaction or unhealthy choices. You might blame your genetics for cravings, lack of time for cooking, or even genetics for slow progress, removing responsibility for your choices and progress.

When you fixate on limits, you are more likely to fall prey to the "all-or-nothing" trap. One missed workout or unhealthy indulgence reinforces the belief that "I cannot do this," leading to discouragement and abandoning the process altogether.

Progress-Focused

In the often-challenging adventure of weight loss, it is easy to get fixated on setbacks and lose sight of the bigger picture. However, cultivating a progress-oriented mindset can be a powerful psychological tool, dramatically increasing your chances of achieving permanent success.

Progress-oriented individuals are the mapmakers of the weight-loss world. They celebrate each conquered hurdle and revel in the expanding landscape of their achievements. Every pound shed, every healthier choice made, fuels their determination.

Focusing on progress shifts the emphasis from the final goal to the smaller steps and achievements along the way. You celebrate increased energy levels, healthier choices, and the development of new skills, regardless of the number on the scale. This constant positive reinforcement fuels motivation and keeps you pushing forward, even when progress feels slow.

When you track your development, you see tangible evidence of your efforts paying off. This builds self-belief, the belief in your own ability to succeed. Seeing how far you have come reinforces your confidence and makes you more likely to tackle future challenges.

Paying attention to improvement helps you bounce back from setbacks more effectively. You view them as temporary deviations, not failures, and utilize them as learning opportunities to refine your approach and stay on track.

Tracking progress fosters a sense of ownership and accountability for your weight loss adventure. You become an active participant in your health, analyzing your choices, adapting your strategies, and taking responsibility for your progress.

Progress tracking provides valuable data on what works and what does not. This empowers you to make informed adjustments to your diet, exercise routine, and lifestyle habits, increasing the effectiveness of your efforts.

Focusing on continuous progress, big or small, reinforces your commitment to change. You see the value of your efforts even when facing challenges, making it easier to maintain motivation and stay on track over the long term.

When you focus growth, you embrace the process as a continuous learning experience. Setbacks become opportunities to refine your approach, experiment with new strategies, and discover what works best for you.

A growth mindset shifts the focus from achieving immediate results to putting in consistent effort and making positive choices. You celebrate the process of learning, growing, and becoming a healthier version of yourself, regardless of the pace of the scale.

Tracking progress allows you to identify areas where you can improve and adapt your approach. You become more flexible, willing to adjust your strategies and routines based on your unique needs and evolving circumstances.

Concentrating on progress is not just about tracking numbers; it is about cultivating a psychological advantage that fuels motivation, resilience, and sustainable change. By celebrating small wins, taking ownership of your weight loss adventure, and embracing a growth mindset, you transform what can be a daunting attempt into a rewarding exploration of self-discovery and personal growth.

Chapter 3
Food-Focused vs. Behavior-Focused

Food-Focused

On the journey to a healthier weight, many stand at a crossroads: the avenue of behavior change or the path of food-centric approaches. Both promise a slimmer you, but the roads they take are vastly different.

Forbidden foods become hyper-palatable and lead to overeating, driven by a complex interplay of psychological and biological factors.

When you restrict certain foods, their perceived value and desirability increase. This is partly due to cognitive dissonance, a mental discomfort arising when our actions (restriction) conflict with our desires (eating the food). Our brain tries to resolve this dissonance by making the restricted food even more appealing.

By constantly thinking about forbidden foods, you keep them at the forefront of your mind, making them more important and triggering cravings. This can be further amplified by external cues like food advertising or the smell of your favorite treats.

When on a diet, you might experience increased stress and negative emotions due to restriction and deprivation. To cope with these, your brain seeks rewarding experiences, like indulging in the forbidden food. This creates a negative feedback loop, where stress triggers cravings, leading to a temporary relief followed by renewed guilt and stress.

Dopamine, a neurotransmitter associated with pleasure and reward, plays a key role in cravings. When you finally give in and eat the forbidden food, it triggers a surge of dopamine, reinforcing the association between the food and pleasure. This strengthens the cravings and makes it harder to resist in the future.

Strict dieting often involves a black-and-white mentality, where one slip-up leads to feelings of failure and complete abandonment of the plan. This triggers the "what the hell" effect, where you justify consuming more of the forbidden food after the initial transgression, believing your progress is already ruined.

Giving in to cravings can lead to a feeling of loss of control and decreased self-belief, the belief in your ability to stick to your goals. This can further weaken your resolve and make it harder to resist cravings in the future.

While food plays a crucial role in weight loss, primarily focusing on it, to the exclusion of other aspects of well-being, can be a detrimental mindset. This "food-centric" approach hinders your chances of achieving permanent success for several psychological reasons.

Fixating on food might lead to neglecting other crucial aspects of health, like physical activity and sleep. These factors significantly impact metabolic processes and influence weight management. Ignoring them creates an unbalanced approach, hindering overall progress.

Obsessing over food overshadows the role of emotional and mental well-being in weight management. Stress, anxiety, and negative self-talk triggers unhealthy eating patterns and sabotage progress. A complete approach prioritizes mental and emotional well-being alongside food choices.

Excessive focus on food can create a fear of foods, leading to restrictive diets and unhealthy relationships with eating.

Fixating on calories, macros, and portions breeds an unhealthy obsession with numbers and restrict spontaneity. This diminishes the joy of eating, ultimately leading to disordered eating patterns. This fosters anxiety, guilt, and a cycle of yo-yo dieting, impacting mental and physical well-being.

A food-centric approach often prioritizes quick fixes and rapid weight loss over long-term sustainable habits. This leads to unhealthy choices and neglects the development of essential skills for permanent change.

Solely focusing on food creates a sense of powerlessness and loss of control, particularly when facing setbacks. This gradually destroys motivation and makes it harder to stay on track when facing challenges.

A food-centric approach often relies on external motivators, like weight-loss goals or societal pressures. This neglects the power of intrinsic motivation, leading to decreased long-term commitment and a tendency to abandon the weight loss adventure altogether.

Fixating on food limits your adventure to a purely physical endeavor. It neglects the potential for personal growth, skill development, and an overall improved quality of life that a holistic approach offers.

Behavior-Focused

The focus often falls on food choices and calorie counting. However, a shift in mindset, from fixating on food to prioritizing behavior, is powerful. For those who champion behavior change, the mantra is "habits, not calories." They focus on building sustainable routines promoting a healthy lifestyle.

Food is a very small part of the weight-loss adventure. All energy and focus should not go into that. There is a much better chance of permanent results when the focus is on long-term habit formation. The strengths lie in addressing the root cause and focus on wellness.

Shifting to behavior emphasizes building new skills and habits into your daily routine, like mindful eating, portion control, and regular physical activity. This focus on process fosters long-term consistency, leading to sustainable change beyond the numbers on the scale.

A behavior-oriented approach empowers you to take ownership of your choices and actions. You focus on developing coping mechanisms for stress, emotional eating, and unhealthy temptations, making you less reliant on external factors or restrictive diets.

Life throws curveballs. Focusing on behavior allows you to adapt your approach to changing circumstances. You learn to navigate social gatherings, manage cravings in healthy ways, and adjust your routines without resorting to quick fixes or harmful deprivation.

Food plays a role, but it is not the sole factor in weight management. Focusing on behavior acknowledges the importance of sleep hygiene, stress management, and emotional well-being. This overall approach creates a foundation for complete health and well-being, not just weight loss.

A behavior-oriented approach encourages mindfulness and self-reflection. You learn to identify triggers, analyze patterns, and develop healthy coping mechanisms for challenges. This builds resilience and a growth mindset, empowering you to bounce back from setbacks and stay on track.

The focus shifts from the limitations of the scale to celebrating every step forward. You acknowledge improved energy levels, better sleep, increased strength, and the development of healthy habits. This fosters self-compassion, motivation, and a sustainable approach to change.

A behavior-oriented approach is a process of personal discovery. You experiment with different routines, learn new skills, and discover what works best for you. This fosters a sense of control and independence, boosting your motivation and commitment to change.

Instead of viewing exercise as a chore, focusing on behavior encourages finding joyful movement options. You try new activities, explore active hobbies, and connect with the pleasure of physical activity. This creates a permanent foundation for sustainable routines you enjoy.

As you master new skills and overcome challenges, your self-confidence grows. You see yourself as capable of making healthy choices and achieving your goals, regardless of temporary setbacks. This newfound confidence fuels your resolve and empowers you to continue on your weight loss adventure.

While food choices matter, focusing on behavior offers a powerful psychological advantage for achieving permanent weight loss success. By building sustainable habits, fostering a holistic perspective, and empowering personal growth, you shift the focus from temporary restrictions to building a healthier, happier you.

Chapter 4
Self-Criticism vs. Self-Compassion

Self-Criticism

The two opposing forces of self-compassion vs. self-criticism have strong influence on dictating whether our weight loss adventure becomes a successful one or a minefield of stumbling blocks.

The fight between self-compassion and self-criticism happens within every mind. The good news is you can choose your champion. By practicing conscious self-talk, actively replacing negative thoughts with kind and understanding affirmations, you cultivate a self-compassionate environment.

Self-criticism might seem like a motivator, a way to push yourself harder and stay on track. However, the opposite is often true. Focusing on self-criticism during weight loss is a major psychological roadblock, significantly decreasing your chances of achieving permanent success.

Constant self-criticism creates a negative feedback loop. Setbacks or perceived failures trigger harsh judgments, leading to discouragement, decreased self-belief, and ultimately, reduced motivation to keep trying.

Harsh self-criticism fosters a fear of failure and judgment. This leads to avoidance behaviors, like skipping workouts or hiding from difficult situations, rather than confronting challenges head-on.

When you constantly beat yourself up, it is difficult to exhibit self-compassion and forgiveness. This makes it harder to bounce back from setbacks, leading to feelings of helplessness and decreased perseverance.

Harsh self-criticism leads to overthinking and excessive analysis. Instead of focusing on action and problem-solving, you get caught in a negative spiral of self-doubt, hindering progress and effective decision-making.

The stress and emotional turmoil caused by self-criticism clouds your judgment and diminishes your ability to focus on your goals. It becomes difficult to prioritize healthy choices and make clear-headed decisions about your well-being.

The emotional drain of self-criticism saps your energy and motivation. You feel overwhelmed and exhausted, making it harder to engage in healthy behaviors and maintain the necessary mental and physical effort for a sustained weight loss adventure.

Self-criticism contributes to stress and negative emotions, which triggers unhealthy coping mechanisms, like emotional eating. This further undermines your progress and creates a detrimental cycle of guilt and self-blame.

When you associate healthy eating with self-criticism and negative judgment, you are less likely to try. This hinders your metabolism, increases stress levels, and ultimately hinders your weight-loss goals.

Constant self-criticism erodes your body image and fosters negative self-perception. This leads to unhealthy expectations and unrealistic goals, setting you up for disappointment and sabotaging your process to a healthier self.

Self-criticism is a powerful force derailing your weight loss adventure. Instead of fostering motivation, it fuels discouragement, hinders progress, and promotes unhealthy behaviors.

Self-Compassion

In the often challenging pursuit of a healthier you, it is tempting to resort to self-criticism when facing hurdles. However, a counterintuitive yet powerful approach lies in cultivating self-compassion. This seemingly soft skill unlocks a wealth of psychological benefits that significantly increase your chances of achieving and maintaining permanent weight-loss success.

Self-compassion replaces negativity with understanding and encouragement. Setbacks become opportunities to learn and grow, fueling motivation to keep trying and adapt your approach. This creates a positive feedback loop sustaining progress over the long term.

When you treat yourself with kindness, you are less likely to fear failure or judgment. This reduces the tendency to avoid challenges and fosters a willingness to experiment, persevere, and bounce back from stumbling blocks.

Self-compassion fosters self-acceptance and appreciation for your efforts, regardless of the numbers on the scale. This builds confidence in your ability to make change and navigate challenges, further bolstering your motivation and commitment.

Self-compassion helps you detach from negative self-judgment and focus on your goals with clarity. You prioritize healthy choices based on your well-being, not self-punishment, making conscious and effective decisions to support your weight-loss adventure.

The emotional burden of self-criticism lifts when you embrace self-compassion. You experience increased energy, improved focus, and a greater capacity to engage in healthy behaviors and maintain the mental and physical effort needed for sustainable change.

Self-compassion creates a safe space for self-reflection and learning. You approach challenges with curiosity and a willingness to understand your triggers and patterns, leading to effective problem-solving and continued progress.

Self-compassion helps you manage stress and negative emotions without resorting to unhealthy coping mechanisms, like emotional eating. You develop healthier ways to navigate challenges, reducing the risk of setbacks and fostering a positive relationship with food.

Self-compassion encourages acceptance and appreciation for your body, regardless of its current state. This positive self-perception helps you set realistic goals, focus on progress, and celebrate your unique adventure without getting caught up in unrealistic expectations or negative self-judgment.

Self-compassion is not a luxury but a powerful tool for achieving permanent weight-loss success. It fuels motivation, enhances goal-oriented actions, and fosters healthy relationships with food and exercise. By choosing kindness and understanding over self-criticism, you embark on a blooming adventure of personal growth and sustainable change.

Chapter 5
Quick Fixes vs. Long-Term Goals

Quick Fixes

In the whirlwind of weight loss, the allure of "quick fixes"—pills, fad diets, extreme exercise routines—can be tempting. However, prioritizing these "shortcuts" over sustainable habits significantly decreases your chances of achieving permanent success.

Quick fixes and fad diets may offer an initial burst, but long-term goals and sustainable habits are the key to crossing the finish line of permanent weight loss, and staying there.

Quick fixes focus on immediate results, neglecting the crucial process of building healthy habits and a sustainable lifestyle. They offer temporary solutions without addressing the underlying factors contributing to weight gain, making future relapse likely.

The promise of rapid weight loss shifts the focus from developing healthy behaviors, like mindful eating and portion control, to achieving a specific number on the scale. This short-term outlook limits the development of essential skills and long-term commitment.

Quick fixes often lead to restrictive dietary patterns or unsustainable exercise regimes, resulting in rapid weight loss followed by rebound weight gain upon returning to normal routines. This creates a disheartening cycle of yo-yo dieting and reinforces a negative self-image.

Quick fixes rarely consider individual health, needs, and preferences. They promote a standardized approach that might be ineffective or even harmful for specific individuals, jeopardizing their overall well-being and long-term health.

The focus on achieving rapid weight loss through quick fixes often neglects the crucial role of mental and emotional well-being in sustainable change. This can lead to increased stress, anxiety, and negative self-image, hindering one's ability to maintain healthy habits.

Fad diets like juice cleanses, keto, fasting, or the grapefruit diet promise rapid weight loss, often with unrealistic claims and restrictive rules. These diets may lead to an initial shedding of pounds, but they are rarely sustainable.

These diets often deprive the body of essential nutrients. Restricting entire food groups or macronutrients can lead to deficiencies in vitamins, minerals, and fiber, impacting your overall health and energy levels and, in the case of fasting, too many nutrients in a short period of time leads to your body not being able to absorb all of it.

Quick fixes often lead to disruption in your metabolism. Crash diets that severely restrict calories can trigger your body to go into starvation mode, slowing down your metabolism and making it harder to lose weight in the long run.

The restrictive nature of quick fixes often leads to rebound weight gain once you return to your normal eating habits. This cycle of weight loss and regain can be detrimental to your physical and mental health.

Long-Term Goals

Instead of chasing the fleeting promises of fad diets, focus on setting realistic and sustainable long-term goals. It is easy to get caught up in the day-to-day battle with the scale. However, shifting your mindset to prioritize long-term goals can be a powerful psychological tool, significantly increasing your chances of achieving permanent weight-loss success.

Long-term goals provide a clear vision of your desired outcome, whether it is improved health, increased energy, or building sustainable habits. This clarity fuels motivation and keeps you focused on the bigger picture, even when faced with challenges.

When you are focused on lasting growth, it goes beyond the limitations of the scale. They include complete improvements in well-being, including physical, mental, and emotional health. This broad perspective promotes a healthier and more sustainable approach to weight management.

It is possible to divide larger objectives into, achievable milestones. This creates a sense of progress and accomplishment, motivating you to persist through temporary setbacks and celebrate incremental victories.

Long-term goals prioritize the development of healthy habits and sustainable processes instead of fixating on immediate results. This fosters resilience as setbacks become opportunities to learn and adapt your approach, not failures derailing your progress.

An understanding that the weight-loss adventure is not always smooth is developed when you have a longer term approach. They allow for occasional slip-ups and unexpected curveballs without triggering self-judgment or discouragement. This fosters a more forgiving and adaptable mindset, aiding in long-term adherence.

It is possible to encourage ongoing learning and exploration when focused on long-term objectives. You gain a deeper understanding of your triggers, effective routines, and personal preferences, empowering you to adjust and refine your approach as you progress.

A deeper connection to your values and motivations is development when you are more focused on results realized in the long run. They align with your desire for a healthier, happier life, fueling intrinsic drive and commitment that goes beyond external pressures or short-term goals.

Focusing on objectives realized over a longer time frame teach you the value of delayed gratification. They require patience and commitment but reward you with permanent gains and a sense of accomplishment that cannot be matched by quick fixes or temporary results.

As you work toward long-term goals, you develop confidence in your ability to make healthy choices and navigate challenges. This self-belief fuels ongoing motivation and empowers you to persevere through difficulties.

While day-to-day tracking and short-term goals have their place, focusing on long-term goals provides a powerful psychological advantage for achieving permanent weight loss success. They offer direction, promote resilience, and cultivate intrinsic motivation.

Chapter 6

Setbacks are a Reason to Quit vs. Setbacks are Learning Opportunities

Setbacks are a Reason to Quit

Setbacks are inevitable. They are the unexpected birthday cake at the office, the late-night stress-fueled pizza binge, or the week-long vacation where your healthy routine falls by the wayside. How you respond to these stumbles is what truly defines your success.

The journey to weight loss is rarely linear. It is a winding road filled with triumphs and stumbles, sunlit stretches and detours into the shadows. And one of the most significant factors determining whether you reach your destination or get lost along the way is your mindset around setbacks.

Framing setbacks as failures triggers feelings of frustration, discouragement, and decreased self-belief. This negative feedback loop gradually destroys motivation, making it harder to bounce back and continue pursuing your goals.

Dwelling on past setbacks develops a fear of future mistakes, creating anxiety and hesitation around healthy choices. This restricts action and progress, leading to lack of progress and potential abandonment of your weight-loss adventure.

Viewing setbacks as complete failures fosters an "all-or-nothing" mentality, where one slip-up invalidates all previous efforts. This rigidity disregards the value of incremental progress and makes it difficult to maintain consistency in the long run.

Viewing setbacks as endings prevents you from analyzing the situation and identifying areas for improvement. This valuable learning opportunity is lost, hindering your ability to adapt your approach and avoid similar obstacles in the future.

Dwelling on setbacks as personal failures reinforces negative self-talk and criticism. This hinders self-compassion, a crucial factor in promoting resilience and bouncing back from challenges.

When setbacks are seen as endings, the larger goals and vision for a healthier you tend to fade into the background. This decreases the power of long-term perspective and weakens your commitment to the continued weight loss adventure.

Viewing setbacks as personal failures can trigger stress and negative emotions, which can lead to unhealthy coping mechanisms like emotional eating. This reinforces unhealthy patterns and distances you from your weight-loss goals.

Focusing on past failures can diminish your confidence in your ability to make healthy choices and achieve your goals. This undermines self-trust and leads to disengagement from the process altogether.

Dwelling on setbacks as definitive failures contributes to negative self-perception and decreased self-worth. This negative association with weight loss further decreases your desire to continue and seek out healthier options.

In short, viewing setbacks as reasons to quit during weight loss significantly decreases your chances of achieving permanent success. This mindset gradually destroys motivation, decreases learning, and promotes unhealthy coping mechanisms.

Setbacks as Learning Opportunities

The weight-loss adventure to a healthier you is rarely smooth sailing. Setbacks are inevitable, but how you choose to approach them can dramatically impact your chances of achieving permanent weight loss success. Shifting your perspective from seeing setbacks as roadblocks to viewing them as valuable learning opportunities unlocks a powerful psychological advantage, paving the way for sustainable change.

When you view setbacks as learning opportunities, you approach them with curiosity and a growth mindset. When you believe in your ability to learn and grow from setbacks, you are more likely to persist through challenges.

When experiencing a setback, it is very important to stop and think about your behavior carefully. Ask questions like "What triggered this setback?" "What could I have done differently?" and "What can I learn from this experience to prevent it from happening again?"

This introspection allows for tweaking of the approach, refining strategies, and building resilience; emerging from the setback stronger, wiser, and better equipped to navigate the challenges ahead.

Framing setbacks as learning opportunities triggers a positive feedback loop. You analyze the situation, identify areas for improvement, and develop strategies to avoid similar obstacles in the future. This proactive approach fosters self-belief and fuels motivation to keep trying.

Viewing setbacks as learning experiences decreases anxiety and encourages exploration. You are less afraid to experiment with new strategies and adapt your approach, making you more resilient and adaptable in the face of future challenges.

Focusing on learning within setbacks allows you to celebrate every step forward, even when the scale does not move as quickly as you would like. This continuous appreciation of progress, big or small, sustains motivation and fosters a positive relationship with your weight-loss adventure.

Setbacks become triggers for deeper reflection. You analyze the situation objectively, identify triggers, and gain valuable insights into your own patterns and preferences. This self-awareness empowers you to make informed choices and refine your approach for better results.

Viewing setbacks as learning experiences encourages you to focus on developing healthy coping mechanisms for stress and negative emotions. You learn alternative ways to navigate challenges, minimizing the risk of resorting to unhealthy behaviors, like emotional eating.

Each setback presents an opportunity to learn and grow. You acquire new skills, refine existing ones, and build a range of healthy strategies for managing challenges. This ongoing development equips you for long-term success and sustainable change.

Viewing setbacks as learning opportunities allows you to be kind and forgiving toward yourself. You understand mistakes are part of the process, and you focus on self-compassion instead of self-criticism. This positive self-talk promotes better emotional well-being and enhances your commitment to your goals.

Embracing a growth mindset fosters the belief you can learn and improve from any experience. This empowers you to take ownership of your weight-loss adventure and confidently navigate challenges, knowing each setback is a stepping stone on your path to success.

Viewing setbacks as opportunities to learn and grow shifts your perception of challenges. They become stepping stones instead of roadblocks, fostering a positive and optimistic outlook fueling your motivation and commitment to long-term change.

Viewing setbacks as learning opportunities is not just a positive perspective; it is a powerful psychological tool that significantly increases your chances of achieving permanent weight-loss success.

Chapter 7

Impulsive Decision-Making vs. Planned Meals and Snacks

Impulsive Decision-Making

Let's face it, the unplanned snack is seductive. The late-night raid on the pantry, the spontaneous office pastry party, the "one slice will not hurt" pizza binge—these are the detours that derail our best intentions. Impulsive eating offers moments of pleasure, a dopamine rush fueled by sugar and fat, but leaves behind a trail of regret and inches on the waist.

Why do we fall prey to these temptations? Our brains, wired for survival, prioritize immediate gratification. That tempting donut promises a quick energy boost, while the thought of prepping healthy meals for the week feels like a distant chore. But here is the catch: indulging in the moment often leads to long-term pain, both physically and mentally.

Impulsive food choices often disregard planned calorie limits and portion control. This throws off your carefully crafted dietary blueprint, leading to overeating and disrupting progress.

Giving in to impulsive cravings derails established routines and healthy habits. You might skip planned workouts, prioritize immediate gratification over nutritious options, and struggle to regain momentum after the slip-up.

Impulsive decisions often stem from emotional triggers or stress, leading to uncontrolled eating patterns and potential emotional eating episodes. This further disrupts progress and reinforces unhealthy coping mechanisms.

Impulsive decisions about food can be fueled by misinterpreting hunger cues. You might mistake boredom, stress, or thirst for hunger, leading to unnecessary food intake and disrupting proper hunger-satiety regulation.

Impulsivity can make you highly susceptible to external food cues like advertisements, social gatherings, or readily available, unhealthy options. You react instinctively to these triggers, often neglecting to make conscious and informed choices.

Emotional states like stress, anxiety, or social pressure can intensify cravings and trigger impulsive food choices. These emotional cravings often lead to seeking highly palatable, calorie-dense options undermining your weight-loss goals.

Frequent impulsive decisions chip away at your commitment to your weight-loss goals. Each slip-up can reinforce feelings of failure and break down your self-belief, making it harder to stay on track and believe in your ability to succeed.

Giving in to impulsive cravings triggers negative self-talk and criticism. You might dwell on mistakes, reinforcing a sense of defeat and restricting your motivation to persevere through challenges.

Impulsive decisions prioritize immediate pleasure over long-term outcomes. You sacrifice the potential health benefits and future successes for temporary taste satisfaction, jeopardizing your overall progress.

Impulsive decision-making about food and meals significantly reduces your chances of achieving permanent weight-loss success. It disrupts routines, amplifies cravings, and gradually destroys your commitment to your goals.

Planned Meals and Snacks

Meal planning and meal prepping are the opposite of impulsive indulgence. It is like having a culinary roadmap for an adventure, ensuring the traveler reaches the weight loss destination without giving in to the roadside distractions.

Taking the time to plan meals and snacks forces intention into what you eat. Choosing the ingredients, portion sizes, and nutritional content leads to taking control of food intake instead of letting hunger dictate choices.

Meal planning eliminates the daily struggle of deciding what to eat. Pre-planned meals and snacks ensures you have healthy options readily available, reduces impulsive decisions, and minimizes the influence of external food cues.

Planning allows you to control food quality and portion sizes with precision. You can tailor meals to your specific needs and goals, preventing overeating and ensuring consistency with your dietary plan.

Planning encourages incorporating diverse and nutritious foods into your diet. You prioritize essential nutrients, balance food groups, and avoid unhealthy options that might tempt you in the moment.

Meal planning creates a structured framework for your day, promoting healthy eating habits and regular mealtimes. This consistent routine improves digestion, regulates hunger cues, and prevents unhealthy snacking patterns.

Knowing what you will eat alleviates the stress and anxiety associated with meal preparation and food choices. This emotional stability enables you to focus on healthy decisions and navigate challenges with greater ease.

Planning promotes autonomy and a sense of control over your weight-loss adventure. You make informed choices about your food, empowering you to take ownership of your health and progress.

Meal planning keeps you aligned with your long-term weight loss goals. You avoid temptations and unhealthy detours, maintaining momentum and preventing derailed progress due to impulsive decisions.

Planning allows you to celebrate small wins, like preparing a healthy meal or sticking to your plan throughout the day. This positive reinforcement enhances motivation and encourages continued commitment to your goals.

Planned meals provide healthy alternatives during times of stress or emotional turmoil. This reduces the reliance on unhealthy coping mechanisms, like emotional eating, and fosters emotional well-being alongside physical health.

Meal planning is not just about portion control; it is about cultivating a mindful and intentional approach on the weight-loss adventure. It empowers you to make informed choices, reduces stress and anxiety, and fosters healthy habits that become the foundation for permanent weight loss.

Chapter 8
Rely on Convenience Food vs. Prepare Healthy Options

Rely on Convenience Food

The drive-thru beckons when we feel our rumbling stomachs and rushed schedules. Instant gratification seems to be the way to go. It appears to be hassle-free. One greasy burger and salty fries in the heat of the moment is an alluring proposition. But for sustainable weight loss, it is a tempting detour on a road best paved with fresh produce and homemade goodness.

Convenience foods are perceived as packaged promises of culinary ease but often come at the cost of long-term health. Hidden sugars, unhealthy fats, and mountains of sodium lurk within those brightly colored wrappers, sabotaging your weight-loss efforts with every bite.

Comfort foods often lack variety and prioritize taste over nutritional content. They tend to be high in unhealthy fats, refined carbohydrates, and sodium, while lacking essential vitamins, minerals, and fiber. This can lead to nutrient imbalances and hinder overall health.

Fast foods often contain hidden sugars and processed ingredients, making it difficult to accurately track calorie intake and manage portion sizes. This lack of transparency undermines informed decision-making and reduces control over your dietary choices.

Pre-packaged foods aimed at convenience are often calorie-dense, meaning they pack a lot of calories into a small volume. This can lead to overconsumption and ruin portion control, ultimately sabotaging weight-loss efforts.

Fast foods encourage quick and unmindful eating patterns. They rely on processed flavors and appealing packaging to trigger impulsive decisions, reducing mindful eating practices and healthy food relationships.

The high sugar and processed ingredients in convenience foods triggers cravings and perpetuates unhealthy eating cycles. This makes it difficult to break free from unhealthy patterns and establish sustainable dietary habits.

Reliance on convenience foods diminishes opportunities to learn cooking skills and gain knowledge about food preparation. This limits your ability to make informed choices, plan healthy meals, and build a sustainable relationship with food.

Consuming primarily convenience foods disconnects you from the emotional and sensory aspects of eating. This leads to a sense of detachment from your health and well-being, reducing long-term motivation and commitment to healthy choices.

Relying on pre-prepared meals diminishes the sense of accomplishment and self-belief that comes from cooking healthy meals from scratch. This can break down motivation and make it harder to persist through challenges on your weight-loss adventure.

Convenience foods prioritize immediate gratification over long-term health benefits. This focus on instant pleasure undermines sustainable change and makes it harder to resist temptations and prioritize long-term well-being.

While convenience foods offer a temporary solution, overreliance on them significantly hinders your chances of achieving permanent weight loss success. They limit nutritional control, promote unhealthy eating habits, and disconnect you from the emotional and well-being aspects of food.

Prepare Healthy Options

So if the fast-food lane leads to frustration and failure, where does the road to sustainable weight loss lie? It begins in your kitchen, with a spoon in hand and a fridge stocked with fresh possibilities. Preparing healthy options offers a wealth of benefits and leads you straight to the path of permanent weight loss.

The journey to a healthier you can be paved with temptations and impulsive decisions. Yet, having readily available healthy options significantly increases your chances of achieving permanent weight loss, not just through physical convenience but by influencing your psychology in powerful ways.

Prepping healthy meals and snacks eliminates the daily struggle of "what to eat?" You make conscious choices in advance, minimizing impulsive decisions in the face of hunger or unhealthy cues, empowering you to stay on track with your goals.

Having healthy options readily available encourages mindful eating practices. You avoid mindlessly grabbing whatever is convenient, allowing for thoughtful portion sizes and savoring each bite with greater awareness.

Preparing healthy choices proactively puts you in control. You build confidence in your ability to navigate challenges and resist temptations, fostering a sense of ownership and commitment to your well-being.

Prepping healthy options creates structure and routine around your eating habits. Regular mealtimes and readily available choices keep you on track, preventing disruptions and maintaining progress over time.

Knowing you have healthy options at your fingertips reduces stress and anxiety about food choices. This emotional stability frees up mental resources, allowing you to focus on other aspects of your well-being and maintain motivation.

Having healthy choices readily available promotes a positive association with food. You approach mealtimes with excitement and anticipation, rather than viewing it as a battle against temptations, making the process more enjoyable and sustainable.

Having healthy options at hand empowers you to resist unhealthy temptations, whether it is late-night cravings or social gatherings. This proactive approach minimizes setbacks and keeps you on the path toward your long-term goals.

Preparing healthy options is a victory in itself. Each prepped meal or snack fuels your motivation and reinforces your commitment. Celebrating these small wins keeps you energized and focused on the bigger picture.

Prepping healthy choices encourages an experimental approach to food. You experiment with new recipes, discover what works best for you, and continuously refine your knowledge about nutrition and portion control, solidifying your long-term success.

Having healthy options readily available during weight loss is not just about convenience; it is about a psychological shift toward empowered choices, mindful eating, and sustainable habits. It reduces stress, fosters self-belief, and fuels your motivation to keep moving forward.

Chapter 9
Lack of Preparation vs. Healthy Alternatives

Lack of Preparation

Winging it might seem more liberating than meticulous planning. However, a lack of preparation during weight loss significantly decreases your chances of achieving permanent success.

With no pre-planned meals or healthy options readily available, the daily question of "what to eat?" becomes a constant battleground. This decision fatigue leads to impulsive choices, often driven by external cues or immediate cravings, undermining healthy intentions.

Lack of preparation leaves you exposed to unhealthy options when hunger strikes. You are more likely to give in to tempting snacks, fast food, or restaurant dishes, destroying your healthy eating efforts and sabotaging progress.

In the moment of hunger, immediate gratification often outweighs long-term goals. Without prepared healthy options, sticking to your dietary plan requires constant willpower and conscious effort, making it harder to prioritize future health benefits over instant pleasure.

Lack of preparation fuels uncertainty and anxiety about food choices. You might worry about finding healthy options on the go or having nothing available at home, leading to stress and increased susceptibility to emotional eating.

Constant challenges in finding healthy options can erode your confidence in your ability to manage your weight loss adventure. This lowers self-belief and motivation, making it harder to persist through challenges and setbacks.

Frequent slip-ups due to lack of preparation can trigger negative self-talk and criticism. This negativity reinforces feelings of failure and lowers your ability to bounce back from setbacks, impacting your overall emotional well-being.

Lack of preparation often leads to erratic mealtimes and mindless snacking. You are more likely to skip meals, overeat when you do eat, and struggle to establish consistent routines crucial for long-term success.

Without preparing and experimenting with healthy options, you miss out on opportunities to develop cooking skills, learn about proper portion control, and discover nutritious foods you enjoy. This reduces your ability to personalize your diet and build sustainable habits tailored to your needs and preferences.

Unplanned eating patterns often disconnect you from the mindful awareness of what you are consuming. You are less likely to be conscious of ingredients, nutritional value, or hunger cues, making it harder to manage your intake and make informed choices for your health.

While lack of preparation may seem like a temporary inconvenience, it has significant psychological consequences that undermine permanent weight-loss success. It weakens decision-making, amplifies stress, and reduces the development of sustainable habits.

Healthy Alternatives

Preparing healthy options is the secret weapon, empowering you to navigate the tumultuous terrain of weight loss with confidence and control.

In the battle of the bulge, having healthy snacks readily available may seem like a mere convenience, but its impact goes far beyond a quick bite, influencing your psychology in remarkable ways, boosting your chances of achieving permanent weight loss success.

Pre-prepared healthy snacks remove the "hangry" scramble for immediate gratification. You avoid impulsive decisions fueled by external cues or cravings, empowering you to make informed choices aligned with your goals.

With accessible healthy alternatives, the enticement of sugary snacks or processed bites loses its power. You minimize reliance on unhealthy options, preventing mindless binges and sticking to your calorie goals with greater ease.

Having healthy snacks on hand encourages mindful eating practices. You slow down, savor each bite, and engage in conscious portion control, preventing overconsumption and promoting a healthier relationship with food.

Ready access to healthy snacks empowers you to navigate hunger triggers and resist temptations. This reinforces your self-belief, bolsters confidence, and strengthens your commitment to your weight-loss adventure.

Knowing you have healthy options at your fingertips alleviates the stress and anxiety around mealtimes and snacking. This emotional stability frees up mental resources, allowing you to focus on other aspects of your well-being and maintaining motivation.

Healthy snacks act as a buffer against emotional triggers and stress-induced cravings. You have a go-to option to soothe negative emotions without resorting to unhealthy coping mechanisms, promoting emotional well-being alongside physical health.

With healthy snacks readily available, you avoid slipping into unhealthy patterns when hunger strikes unexpectedly. This consistent adherence to your dietary plan keeps you on track, minimizing setbacks and preventing derailment from your long-term goals.

Experimenting with diverse and delicious healthy snacks expands your culinary horizons. You discover new favorite options, learn about portioning and nutrient content, and solidify your commitment to a sustainable, enjoyable approach to healthy eating.

Having healthy snacks on hand reframes your perception of snacking. It becomes a source of fuel and nourishment, rather than a guilty indulgence. This fosters a positive relationship with food, promoting intuitive eating habits and long-term dietary adherence.

Having healthy snacks readily available during weight loss is not just about instant access to fuel; it is about bolstering your psychological armor. It empowers informed choices, fosters resilience, and supports long-term goals.

Chapter 10

Relying on Willpower vs. Relying on Removing Cravings

Relying on Willpower

In the weight-loss arena you have two completely opposite approaches: the one relying on willpower to hack and slash through all the temptation coming your way or the gracefully and effortlessly bypassing of the alluring traps with honed intuition and strategic moves.

Willpower. That noble knight we are told to summon whenever desire beckons, but relying solely on it is like charging uphill through quicksand—exhausting, frustrating, and ultimately futile. Every craving resisted is a battle won, yes, but at what cost? Constant tension, deprivation, and an ever-present risk of a binge-eating counteroffensive. This mental fatigue often leads to eventual surrender, plunging you back into the cycle of restriction and rebellion.

Every decision about food, portion sizes, and cravings requires willpower. This constant effort exhausts your mental resources, leading to decision fatigue and reducing your ability to make good choices consistently.

With your willpower reserves depleted, you become more susceptible to external cues and cravings. You are more likely to make impulsive decisions, give in to temptations, and stray from your healthy intentions.

Constant reliance on willpower creates a pressure-cooker environment. This leads to stress, negative self-talk, and decreased motivation, further eroding your resolve and making consistent healthy choices feel like an uphill battle.

Over reliance on willpower often leads to a rigid or "all-or-nothing" approach to weight loss. One slip-up can trigger negative self-assessments and spiral into unhealthy guilt or discouragement.

Rigid adherence to strict rules and willpower-driven choices can reduce your ability to adapt to changing situations or experiment with new healthy options. This makes it difficult to build sustainable habits fitting your evolving needs and preferences.

Constant control and self-deprivation disconnects you from the pleasure and enjoyment of food. This leads to a negative relationship with food, creating frustration and hindering long-term adherence to healthy changes.

Willpower focuses primarily on resisting temptations and meeting short-term goals. This overshadows the long-term vision of building sustainable habits and improving overall health.

Solely relying on willpower keeps you in a reactive state, constantly battling against challenges. This hinders your sense of ownership and confidence in your ability to manage your weight loss adventure independently.

Negative self-talk and reliance on willpower often lead to a lack of self-compassion after slip-ups. This reduces your ability to bounce back from setbacks, learn from experiences, and maintain positive reinforcement strategies.

While willpower has a role to play in weight loss, relying solely on it sets you up for failure. It drains your mental resources, fosters rigid and unsustainable habits, and undermines your long-term goals and self-belief.

Relying on Removing Cravings

While the allure of eliminating cravings entirely during weight loss may seem like a shortcut, focusing on managing them through strategic food choices significantly increases your chances of achieving permanent success. This shift in mindset has less to do with the myth of a limited willpower reserve and more to do with understanding the underlying psychology of cravings and our relationship with food.

Cravings are often triggered by a complex interplay of biological, emotional, and environmental cues. Focusing solely on eliminating them ignores these underlying factors, making long-term management difficult.

Choosing nutrient-rich and fiber-dense foods regulates blood sugar and promotes satiety, reducing the frequency and intensity of cravings triggered by hunger or hormonal fluctuations.

Paying attention to internal cues like hunger and fullness, slowing down during meals, and savoring each bite helps break the automatic association between certain foods and cravings, fostering a healthier relationship with food.

Shifting focus from elimination to management empowers you to identify triggers, develop healthy coping mechanisms (like walking or doing a hobby you enjoy), and navigate cravings without resorting to impulsive or unhealthy choices.

Viewing occasional cravings as normal and accepting them as part of the process promotes self-compassion and reduces stress. This reduces the likelihood of resorting to emotional eating or giving up on your goals altogether.

Acknowledging and celebrating even small successes in managing cravings reinforces positive behavior, boosts motivation, and fosters a sense of progress, keeping you committed to your long-term goals.

Exploring new and healthy recipes, incorporating diverse ingredients, and finding nutritious alternatives to satisfying your taste preferences reduces reliance on specific foods that might trigger intense cravings.

Eliminating certain foods entirely can backfire, leading to intense cravings and ultimately fueling binge episodes. Choosing nutrient-rich options as your primary focus allows for occasional indulgences without triggering the cycle of restriction and overconsumption.

Viewing food as fuel and nourishment for both your body and mind cultivates a positive relationship with eating. This reduces the tendency to use food as a coping mechanism for stress or emotional triggers, making healthy choices more naturally sustainable.

By focusing on managing cravings through strategic food choices, mindful eating practices, and self-compassion, you build sustainable habits, navigate challenges with resilience, and redefine your relationship with food in a way that supports permanent weight-loss success.

Chapter 11
Quit and Start Over All the Time vs. Consistent

Quit and Start Over All the Time

The allure of a fresh start often fuels the cycle of quitting and restarting during weight loss. However, this pattern, also known as yo-yo dieting, significantly decreases your chances of achieving permanent success.

The frequent cycle of starting, stopping, and starting can lead to a string of setbacks. This fuels negative self-talk, lowering your confidence and belief in your ability to maintain healthy habits.

Each "quit" erases the progress made during the "start" phase. The constant back-and-forth disrupts routines, hinders goal setting, and makes it harder to build sustainable momentum toward your long-term vision.

The temporary nature of "starts" can foster a detached approach to your weight-loss adventure. You might feel less invested in making long-term changes, reducing your commitment and sense of ownership in achieving your goals.

The yo-yo cycle creates a rollercoaster of weight fluctuations. This puts stress on your metabolism and hormonal system, making it harder to regulate hunger cues, control cravings, and maintain energy levels.

Frequent weight regains after dieting can lead to "metabolic adaptation," where your body adapts to store more fat in anticipation of future restrictions. This makes losing weight even more challenging in the long run.

The yo-yo cycle is linked to increased risks of various health issues, including diabetes, heart disease, and even depression. The constant fluctuations in weight and stress on your body take a toll on your overall well-being.

The "start" phase often emphasizes rapid weight loss through restrictive diets or intense exercise routines. This focus on short-term results neglects the importance of building sustainable habits and making long-term lifestyle changes.

The on-again, off-again approach lowers the development of mindful eating practices and understanding of healthy food choices. This makes it difficult to maintain healthy habits or make informed decisions outside of the "start" phases.

The frequent resets in the yo-yo cycle can disconnect you from your body's natural hunger and fullness cues. This dependence on external control mechanisms, like restrictive diets, lowers your ability to develop intuitive eating habits and listen to your internal signals.

Quitting and restarting during weight loss may seem like a temporary setback, but it significantly undermines your chances of achieving permanent success. It gradually destroys motivation, disrupts your body's balance, and hinders the development of sustainable habits.

Consistent

In the whirlwind of weight-loss efforts, the allure of quick fixes and drastic changes can be tempting. However, the secret to permanent success lies in a seemingly simple yet powerful concept: consistent effort.

Every consistent action, every healthy choice, adds a brick to the foundation of your progress. This sustained effort reinforces your self-belief, building confidence in your ability to maintain these changes over time.

Consistency acknowledges that setbacks are inevitable, but not derailments. It allows you to view them as learning opportunities, fostering resilience and preventing discouragement from temporary bumps in the road.

Focusing on consistent effort shifts the focus from grand goals to everyday wins. Celebrating each healthy meal, workout completed, or craving successfully managed reinforces positive behavior and fuels ongoing motivation.

Healthy behaviors get ingrained in your everyday routine when you are consistent. Regular mealtimes, planned exercise sessions, and mindful eating practices become part of your routine, reducing decision fatigue and promoting effortless adherence.

Making a constant effort helps you become more aware of your body's signals of hunger and fullness, which promotes mindful eating. This reduces emotional dependence on food, promotes intuitive choices, and fosters a healthy relationship with eating.

Being dependable recognizes that weight loss is not always a straight line. It allows you to embrace progress over perfection, focusing on maintaining the overall trend of healthy choices, even with occasional indulgences or slip-ups.

When healthy choices become habitual, you free up mental resources previously spent on constant thinking about food and exercise. This reduces stress and improves overall cognitive function.

Constancy empowers you to navigate challenging situations and emotional triggers with healthier coping mechanisms. You are less likely to resort to emotional eating or unhealthy habits as a form of stress relief.

Steady effort promotes a balanced and sustainable approach to weight loss. You avoid the highs and lows of restrictive diets and compulsive exercise, fostering a healthy mind-body connection and reducing the risk of disordered eating patterns.

While consistency may seem like a simple concept, its impact on your weight-loss adventure is profound. It reinforces confidence, builds sustainable habits, and promotes emotional well-being.

Chapter 12
Skipping Meals vs. Regular Balanced Meals

Skipping Meals

While skipping meals might seem like a quick way to cut calories and shed pounds, it significantly decreases your chances of achieving permanent weight loss. This goes beyond the simple physics of calories in and out, delving into the complex psychology of how skipping meals impacts your mindset and behaviors.

Skipping meals puts your body into a "conservation mode," slowing down your metabolism to conserve energy. This can make it harder to burn calories and achieve weight-loss goals in the long run.

Missing meals leads to fluctuating blood sugar levels, triggering cravings for sugary or high-fat foods. This cycle of highs and lows makes it harder to resist temptations and maintain consistent energy levels throughout the day.

Skipping meals disrupts the delicate balance of hormones like insulin and leptin, responsible for regulating hunger and satiety. This can lead to increased hunger pangs, decreased satiety, and ultimately, overconsumption later in the day.

When you are hungry, your willpower and decision-making abilities take a hit. You are more likely to make impulsive choices, grabbing quick and unhealthy snacks instead of sticking to your planned meals.

With an empty stomach, you are more vulnerable to external cues and cravings. The sight or smell of tempting foods becomes almost irresistible, leading to unhealthy binges or slip-ups from your dietary plan.

Frequent hunger pangs and cravings can be discouraging. Skipping meals can lead to negative self-talk and lowers your confidence in your ability to manage your weight loss adventure effectively.

Skipping meals disconnects you from your body's natural hunger and fullness signals. This can lead to emotional eating, using food to cope with stress or negative emotions, reducing the development of healthy coping mechanisms.

The tendency to skip meals snowballs into restrictive eating patterns, causing anxiety and unhealthy fixations on certain foods or calorie count. This ultimately leads to disordered eating behaviors or unwanted binges.

The frustration and setbacks associated with skipping meals fosters a negative relationship with food and weight loss. You might view it as a constant battle or punishment, lowering your overall well-being and motivation.

Skipping meals may offer a temporary illusion of progress, but it sets you up for failure in the long run. It disrupts your metabolism, weakens your willpower, and promotes unhealthy eating habits and relationships with food.

Regular Balanced Meals

In the quest for a healthier you, skipping meals might seem like a shortcut, but eating regular, balanced meals acts as a powerful psychological ally, significantly increasing your chances of achieving permanent weight-loss success.

Regular meals keep your metabolism humming, optimizing calorie burning and preventing the body from going into "conservation mode." This translates to more efficient nutrient use and sustained energy levels throughout the day.

Consistent meals maintain balanced blood sugar levels, minimizing cravings, preventing energy crashes, and reducing the urge for sugary or unhealthy snacks. This stability keeps you focused and in control of your choices.

Regular meals stabilize the delicate balance of hormones like insulin and leptin, responsible for hunger and satiety. This ensures proper signaling for hunger and fullness, preventing overconsumption and promoting mindful eating.

When you are well fueled, your willpower and decision-making abilities stay sharp. You are less likely to make impulsive choices driven by hunger pangs, making it easier to stick to your planned meals and avoid unhealthy temptations.

Regular meals stabilize your blood sugar and minimize cravings, preventing you from becoming vulnerable to external cues or irresistible urges for unhealthy foods. This empowers you to stay on track with your dietary goals and resist emotional eating triggers.

Consistent meals fuel your body and mind, keeping you energized and motivated. With regular nourishment, you are more likely to feel capable and confident in your ability to manage your weight-loss adventure effectively.

Regular meals help you relearn and listen to your body's natural hunger and fullness signals. This fosters intuitive eating practices, promoting healthy relationships with food and preventing emotional reliance on it.

Balanced meals provide a structured framework for making healthy and diverse food choices. This ensures you receive essential nutrients while minimizing overconsumption of unhealthy options.

Regular meals eliminate the need for extreme calorie restriction or unhealthy eating patterns. This promotes a sustainable and enjoyable approach to weight loss, preventing the development of disordered eating behaviors or negative associations with food.

Eating regular, balanced meals is not just about providing your body with fuel; it is about setting yourself up for psychological success on your weight-loss adventure. It optimizes your body's functions, strengthens your willpower, and cultivates a healthy relationship with food.

Chapter 13
Mindless Snacking vs. Mindful Eating

Mindless Snacking

Mindless eating, the hasty feast, is fueled by autopilot. Eating out of habit, boredom, or emotional triggers, oblivious to the symphony of flavors and sensations unfolding on our palates. Each bite becomes a blur, portions morph into monsters, and portion awareness vanishes like mist in the morning.

Mindless eating often leads to overconsumption, exceeding the body's needs before we even realize it. Lost in our thoughts, we devour an entire pie, oblivious to the ballooning numbers on the calorie counter.

While indulging in a tasty treat might seem harmless, frequent mindless snacking significantly decreases your chances of achieving permanent weight-loss success. It goes beyond the simple calorie count, delving into the complex psychology of how snacking habits impact your mindset and behaviors.

Constantly making decisions about snacks depletes your mental resources, leading to decision fatigue. You are more likely to make impulsive choices based on external cues or immediate cravings, neglecting your planned dietary goals.

Mindless snacking often involves distracted eating, where you consume food without paying attention to the quantity or quality. This leads to overconsumption and lowers your ability to manage portion sizes effectively.

Frequent slip-ups due to mindless snacking breaks down your self-belief and confidence in your ability to manage your weight-loss adventure. This leads to discouragement and decreased motivation to maintain healthy habits.

Mindless snacking disconnects you from your body's natural hunger and satiety cues. You might mistake boredom, stress, or even thirst for hunger, leading to unnecessary food intake and lowering your ability to develop intuitive eating practices.

Snacking becomes a coping mechanism for stress, anxiety, or negative emotions. This emotional reliance on food leads to unhealthy patterns and sabotages your weight loss efforts.

Mindless snacking often involves unhealthy, processed foods, contributing to a negative relationship with food. You might view it as a source of comfort or reward, rather than a source of nourishment and fuel.

Mindless snacking prevents you from practicing mindful eating habits, like savoring each bite, recognizing portion sizes, and appreciating the nutritional value of your food. This lowers your ability to build sustainable changes and long-term healthy habits.

Frequent snacking throws off your meal schedule and disrupts your planned dietary routines. This makes it harder to maintain consistency and track your overall food intake effectively.

The cycle of mindless snacking, slip-ups, and self-criticism erodes your motivation and commitment to your weight-loss goals. This leads to a feeling of being overwhelmed and discourages you from continuing your weight-loss adventure.

While a mindful snack here and there may not derail your progress, frequent mindless snacking significantly hinders your chances of achieving permanent weight loss. It weakens your control mechanisms, disrupts hunger cues and emotional regulation, and makes it difficult to build sustainable habits.

Mindful Eating

Mindful eating, the deliberate feast, is an act of self-awareness. It is about engaging with food on all levels, transforming each meal into a mindful adventure.

In the pursuit of a healthier you, while strict diets and calorie counting might seem like the silver bullet, embracing mindful eating stands as a powerful psychological ally, significantly increasing your chances of achieving permanent weight-loss success. It goes beyond simply watching your portions; it is about tuning into your body's wisdom and cultivating a healthy relationship with food.

Being mindful of your body's natural cues of hunger and fullness is part of mindful eating. You learn to distinguish true hunger from emotional cravings, boredom, or thirst, preventing unnecessary food intake and fostering intuitive eating practices.

Eating with awareness slows down your pace, allowing you to savor each bite and register satiety cues before overindulging. This promotes portion control and prevents mindless consumption based on external cues or habits.

You are more conscious of the feelings, ideas, and triggers that influence your dietary decisions when you are more aware of what you are eating. This self-understanding empowers you to make informed decisions aligned with your long-term goals and well-being.

Mindful eating engages your conscious mind, reducing decision fatigue and impulsive choices. You are better equipped to navigate temptations, say no to unhealthy options, and stick to your planned dietary goals with greater ease.

You may recognize and deal with the emotional triggers that frequently result in unhealthful eating habits by practicing mindful eating. This reduces your reliance on food as a coping mechanism for stress or negative emotions, promoting healthier stress-management strategies.

Eating mindfully fosters a non-judgmental approach to food and setbacks. You learn to accept occasional slip-ups as part of the process, avoiding negative self-talk and maintaining motivation to stay on track.

Being conscious of your eating encourages you to focus on the sensory experience of food, savor flavors, and appreciate the nourishment it provides. This transforms your relationship with food from a source of guilt or control to one of mindful enjoyment and well-being.

Being fully present while you are having a meal allows you to make conscious food choices based on nutritional value, personal preferences, and hunger cues. This leads to a naturally balanced and diverse diet, ensuring you receive the nutrients your body needs without depriving yourself of the foods you enjoy.

This mindfulness becomes integrated into your daily life, creating sustainable routines around mealtimes and mindful snacking. This consistency reduces the need for strict plans or rigid rules, making your weight-loss adventure enjoyable and adaptable.

Conscious eating is not just a trendy term; it is a powerful tool for rewiring your relationship with food and transforming your approach to weight loss. By paying attention to your body's wisdom, you unlock the secrets of intuitive eating, strengthen your control mechanisms, and build sustainable habits for permanent success.

Chapter 14
Lack of Support vs. Mentor Support

Lack of Support

While individual determination is crucial, lack of support during weight loss significantly decreases your chances of achieving permanent success. This goes beyond simply needing someone to cheer you on; it is about the psychological impact of navigating challenges alone.

Without a support system, the internal pressure to stay on track reduces. The lack of external accountability leads to slip-ups, discouragement, and a weakening of your commitment to your goals.

Facing cravings, setbacks, and social pressures alone is overwhelming. Without reliable support to encourage you through challenging situations, you are more likely to give in to temptations and stray from your healthy choices.

The adventure of weight loss is filled with ups and downs. Without mentor support to provide positive reinforcement and a different perspective, negative self-talk and self-doubt easily creeps in, eroding your motivation and confidence.

Weight loss is an emotionally challenging adventure. Without support to share your struggles and anxieties, stress levels increase, triggering unhealthy coping mechanisms, like emotional eating or neglecting self-care.

Lack of support leads to feelings of isolation and loneliness, further fueling negative emotions and lowering your overall well-being. This creates a vicious cycle where emotional strain sabotages progress on your weight-loss adventure.

The pressure of navigating challenges alone makes it harder to practice self-compassion and mindfulness. Without a supportive voice reminding you of your progress and cheering you on through setbacks, you are more likely to be harsh on yourself and derail your progress.

Having the right support system helps establish healthy routines and make them more enjoyable. Without someone to share meal ideas with or simply talk to about your goals, it can be harder to stay consistent and motivated in the long run.

Mentor support is a valuable source of information, tips, and shared experiences. Lacking this resource limits your knowledge about healthy habits, effective strategies, and potential challenges, hindering your ability to make informed decisions and adapt to obstacles.

While independent strength is admirable, a strong support system plays a crucial role in achieving and maintaining permanent weight-loss success. It strengthens your motivation, helps manage stress and emotions, and facilitates the formation of sustainable habits.

Mentor Support

With a supportive mentor beside you, weight loss transforms from a solo expedition into a collaborative adventure. A mentor becomes the cheerleader, the confidant, and accountability partner. They celebrate the victories, empathize with the struggles, and offer unwavering encouragement when doubt creeps in. The person trying to make healthy eating changes, with the mentor's shoulder to lean on, feels empowered to overcome challenges and persevere.

In the quest for a healthier you, while self-determination is vital, enlisting the support of a mentor significantly increases your chances of achieving permanent weight-loss success. It goes beyond simple advice; it is about harnessing the psychological power of guidance, accountability, and personalized understanding.

A mentor tailors their approach to your unique needs and goals, providing individualized guidance and support keeping you motivated and engaged. This personalized plan fosters a sense of purpose and strengthens your commitment to permanent change.

With a mentor watching your back, the internal pressure to stay on track intensifies. Regular check-ins, progress monitoring, and constructive feedback create a system of accountability encouraging consistency and progress.

A mentor celebrates your victories, no matter how small, providing constant encouragement and positive reinforcement. This boosts your confidence, reinforces healthy behaviors, and increases your motivation to keep moving forward.

Weight loss can be emotionally challenging. A mentor offers a safe space to share your struggles, anxieties, and setbacks. This emotional support helps you manage stress, find healthy coping mechanisms, and navigate challenges with greater resilience.

With a mentor's guidance, you learn to practice self-compassion and challenge negative self-talk. This shift in perspective helps you manage setbacks constructively, maintain a positive outlook, and stay focused on your long-term goals.

A mentor guides you in developing mindfulness practices and cultivating emotional awareness. This enables you to identify triggers, understand your emotions, and make conscious choices aligning with your well-being rather than succumbing to emotional eating or impulses.

A mentor with specialized knowledge and experience provides valuable insights and practical strategies tailored to your specific needs and challenges. This access to expertise accelerates your learning curve and increases your success rate.

With a mentor's guidance, you establish healthy routines, create a supportive environment, and develop sustainable habits fitting your lifestyle. This personalized approach ensures permanent change beyond superficial quick fixes.

When progress stalls, a mentor helps you identify underlying issues, adjust your approach, and overcome plateaus. This ongoing support promotes encouragement, keeps you focused on solutions, and ensures consistent progress toward your goals.

A mentor's support is not just an addition; it is a powerful catalyst for permanent weight-loss success. It strengthens your motivation, enhances coping mechanisms, and accelerates knowledge and habit formation.

Chapter 15
Avoid Self-Monitoring vs. Tracking Yourself

Avoid Self-Monitoring

To avoid self-tracking is like navigating the jungle blindfolded. It leaves you an easy target for pitfalls and hidden dangers.

While the idea of escaping the hassle of tracking and measuring may be tempting, avoiding self-monitoring during weight loss significantly decreases your chances of achieving permanent success and undermines your accountability. This goes beyond simply needing numbers on a scale or a food diary; it is about the psychological impact of staying in the dark about your progress and choices.

Without self-monitoring, you miss valuable feedback on your efforts. You lose sight of the progress you have made, hindering your ability to celebrate victories and learn from setbacks. This disconnect can diminish motivation and make it harder to stay focused on your goals.

Avoiding self-monitoring keeps you in the dark about your actual food intake, exercise routines, and lifestyle habits. This lack of awareness makes it difficult to identify areas for improvement or recognize patterns that might be sabotaging your progress.

Without data or objective feedback, your perception of progress becomes skewed. You might overestimate your efforts or underestimate challenges, leading to unrealistic expectations and eventual disappointment, ultimately sabotaging your long-term success.

Avoiding self-monitoring removes a layer of external pressure and accountability. This leads to less consistent efforts, increased slip-ups, and a weaker commitment to your goals in the long run.

Without self-monitoring, you might miss early warning signs of setbacks or unhealthy patterns. This makes it harder to address challenges proactively and adapt your approach as needed, reducing your ability to overcome obstacles.

Avoiding self-monitoring fuels denial and a tendency to make excuses for unhealthy choices. This lack of self-awareness lowers your ability to take responsibility for your actions and make conscious changes aligning with your goals.

Self-monitoring provides valuable data for reflection and learning. By avoiding it, you miss the chance to identify triggers, understand your eating patterns, and adjust your approach based on your observations.

Without self-monitoring, you might overlook subtle patterns and emotional triggers leading to unhealthy choices. This lack of awareness hinders your ability to develop coping mechanisms and build sustainable eating habits.

Blindly navigating your weight-loss adventure can be disheartening. Without data or feedback to track your progress, it can be challenging to stay motivated and maintain a positive outlook, ultimately impacting your long-term commitment.

Avoiding self-monitoring during weight loss may seem like an escape from stress, but it comes at a significant cost. It hinders your awareness of progress, weakens your accountability, and limits your ability to learn and adapt. Remember, permanent change thrives on information and self-awareness.

Tracking Yourself

Self-tracking sheds light on your path, empowering you to navigate toward success.

Tracking your intake and activity levels reveals the truth about habits, getting the opportunity to scrutinize personal behavior to pinpoint patterns and identify calorie-rich culprits, gaining newfound control over the weight-loss adventure.

In the quest for a healthier you, while willpower is crucial in the beginning stages, embracing self-tracking significantly increases your chances of achieving permanent weight-loss success and encourages genuine accountability. It goes beyond a simple log of numbers; it is about harnessing the psychological power of awareness, data-driven insights, and personalized adjustments.

Self-tracking provides invaluable feedback on your efforts. You witness the progress you have made, celebrate milestones, and learn from setbacks. This data-driven insight fosters motivation, strengthens your commitment, and keeps you focused on your long-term goals.

Tracking reveals patterns in your food intake, exercise routines, and lifestyle choices. This self-awareness empowers you to identify areas for improvement, adjust your approach based on data, and make informed decisions aligning with your goals.

Data empowers you to set realistic expectations and objectively evaluate your progress. This reduces the risk of unrealistic goals or discouragement, maintaining a positive and optimistic outlook on your weight-loss adventure. Data empowers you to set realistic expectations and objectively evaluate your progress. This reduces the risk of unrealistic goals or discouragement, maintaining a positive and optimistic outlook on your weight-loss adventure.

Self-tracking creates a self-imposed pressure to stay on track. The act of recording your choices reinforces accountability, leading to more consistent efforts, greater adherence to your goals, and a stronger sense of responsibility for your progress.

Tracking allows you to identify potential challenges and unhealthy patterns early on. This proactive approach gives you the power to address issues before they derail your progress, ensuring smooth navigation on your weight-loss adventure.

Recording your choices makes it difficult to deny your actions or rationalize unhealthy choices. This promotes self-ownership of your process, fostering a commitment to making conscious changes for permanent success.

Self-tracking provides valuable data for reflection and ongoing self-evaluation. By analyzing your patterns, you gain insights into triggers, understand your personal eating landscape, and adjust your approach based on your observations.

Tracking reveals your unique patterns and responses, facilitating the development of personalized strategies catering to your specific needs and challenges. This data-driven approach optimizes your weight-loss adventure for permanent success.

Seeing evidence of your progress in numbers and data can be incredibly motivating. Self-tracking allows you to celebrate achievements, acknowledge milestones, and maintain a positive outlook throughout your process, fueling your commitment and resilience.

Self-tracking is not just a chore; it is an impressive tool for empowerment and self-discovery. It elevates your awareness, strengthens accountability, and encourages continuous learning and adaptation.

Chapter 16
Poor Sleep Hygiene vs. Prioritizing Adequate Sleep

Poor Sleep Hygiene

Skimping on sleep, like swimming with fogged-up goggles, distorts your perception and throws you off course.

Neglecting proper sleep hygiene during weight loss significantly decreases your chances of achieving permanent success. This goes beyond simply feeling tired; it's about the complex psychological impact sleep has on your hormones, hunger cues, and self-control, ultimately sabotaging your weight loss efforts.

Poor sleep throws off your body's production of leptin (the satiety hormone) and ghrelin (the hunger hormone). This can lead to increased hunger cravings, particularly for unhealthy, processed foods, making it harder to stick to your planned meals and food goals.

Sleep deprivation increases cortisol, a stress hormone linked to increased abdominal fat storage and unhealthy food choices. This hormonal imbalance can heighten cravings, promote emotional eating, and make it harder to resist temptations, sabotaging your progress.

Lack of sleep impairs your brain's prefrontal cortex, responsible for executive function and self-control. This cognitive fatigue makes it harder to resist impulsive cravings, leading to poor food choices and lowering your ability to make conscious decisions about your diet.

Sleep deprivation blurs your body's natural hunger and satiety cues. You might mistake fatigue or boredom for hunger, leading to unnecessary food intake and lowering your ability to intuitively regulate your food intake.

When sleep-deprived, you are more susceptible to emotional eating and using food as a coping mechanism for stress or negative emotions. This can derail your diet and lead to unhealthy patterns that sabotage your weight-loss goals.

Sleep deprivation can break down your motivation and commitment to your weight loss goals. With low energy and cognitive fatigue, you are more likely to slip up, skip workouts, and find it harder to consistently maintain healthy habits.

Poor sleep can increase negative self-talk and feelings of discouragement, especially after slip-ups or setbacks. This negative self-image can hinder your long-term commitment and make it harder to bounce back from challenges.

Chronic sleep deprivation creates a vicious cycle. It disrupts your hormones, weakens control mechanisms, and reduces motivation, ultimately increasing the risk of relapsing into unhealthy patterns and sabotaging your long-term weight management goals.

Prioritizing proper sleep hygiene during weight loss is not just about feeling well-rested; it is about optimizing your body's internal systems, strengthening your resilience to temptations, and setting yourself up for sustainable success. Remember, permanent change requires an overall approach.

Prioritize Adequate Sleep

Prioritizing adequate sleep during weight loss significantly increases your chances of achieving permanent success. This goes beyond feeling energized; it is about the intricate psychological impact sleep has on your hormones, hunger cues, and mental resilience, ultimately harmonizing your mind and body for sustained progress.

Adequate sleep balances leptin (the satiety hormone) and ghrelin (the hunger hormone), minimizing cravings for unhealthy, fatty, and sugary foods. This internal balance keeps you feeling naturally satisfied, making it easier to stick to your planned meals and resist impulsive snacking.

Sleep reduces cortisol, a stress hormone linked to fat storage and unhealthy eating. This hormonal harmony stabilizes your metabolism, prevents emotional eating triggers, and empowers you to make conscious food choices aligned with your goals.

Rest boosts your prefrontal cortex, the brain region responsible for executive function and impulse control. This mental focus and willpower equip you to resist temptations, make informed decisions about your diet, and stay on track even when presented with external cues.

Adequate sleep sharpens your body's natural hunger and satiety cues. You can clearly distinguish between true hunger and emotional triggers, ensuring you eat only when your body needs fuel, not as a coping mechanism.

Rest strengthens your emotional resilience, making you less susceptible to using food as a coping mechanism for stress or negative emotions. This emotional stability prevents unhealthy eating patterns and keeps you focused on your weight-loss goals, even during challenging times.

A well-rested mind is a clear and determined mind. Adequate sleep strengthens your commitment to your weight-loss goals, keeps you energized and motivated, and helps you maintain consistent healthy habits for the long haul.

Sleep fosters optimism and reduces negative self-talk, especially after setbacks. This mental resilience allows you to bounce back from challenges, learn from mistakes, and stay focused on your long-term vision.

By optimizing your hormones, strengthening your willpower, and boosting your emotional resilience, adequate sleep significantly reduces the risk of relapses and unhealthy weight regain. This holistic approach equips you for long-term weight management and sustained success.

Prioritizing adequate sleep during weight loss is not just about recharging your batteries; it is about harmonizing your body's internal symphony, strengthening your mental resilience, and creating sustainable habits for lifelong well-being.

Chapter 17

Fixating on the Scale vs. Celebrating Non-scale Victories

Fixating on the Scale

Being fixated on the scale as a weight-loss tool is a fascinating and self-defeating contradiction. While the number on the scale might seem like a concrete, objective measure of progress, it can actually sabotage your weight-loss efforts in multiple ways.

Fixating on the scale narrows your focus from healthy habits and overall well-being to a single, ever-changing number. This obsession overshadows the positive changes you are making, leading to discouragement and frustration.

Every fluctuation on the scale becomes a source of intense emotions, with even small gains triggering feelings of failure and low self-esteem, while losses may lead to unhealthy celebratory binges, which leaves you ashamed, guilty, and disappointed in yourself. This emotional fluctuation interferes with long-term motivation and consistency.

The scale does not reflect the complex combination of factors influencing weight, such as muscle gain, water retention, or hormonal fluctuations. Focusing solely on the number ignores these crucial elements, leading to unrealistic expectations and misinterpretations of progress, especially when we think we can influence it.

Comparing your scale numbers to others, especially through social media, can be a recipe for disappointment. Individual bodies respond differently to weight-loss approaches, and obsessing over comparisons sets you up for frustration and potentially harmful competition.

The pressure to see a lower number on the scale leads to unhealthy restrictive eating and excessive exercise, potentially triggering disordered eating habits and undermining your physical and mental health.

The scale-centric view can shift your focus from building sustainable healthy habits for the long term to quick fixes and temporary weight-loss tactics that are ultimately unsustainable and detrimental to your well-being.

We want to be in control of our lives, most of all our weight. We would love to think that is the number down on the scale, but it is one thing we cannot control, and when it does not do what we hoped it would do, it sets us into a tailspin where we want to give up immediately and pull that box of chocolates closer to keep us company while we lick our wounds.

Fixating on the scale fosters a narrow, number-driven approach to weight loss. Every pound lost becomes a triumph, every ounce gained a devastating setback. This emotional roller coaster is unsustainable, leading to discouragement, self-blame, and ultimately, a return to old, unhealthy habits.

Celebrating Non-scale Victories

Instead, we must shift our focus to the non-scale victories, the often-overlooked milestones that signal true progress and sustainable change. These victories whisper not in a number but in a whisper of energy, a newfound strength, a shift in mindset.

Focusing on non-scale victories as your primary measure of progress in weight loss offers a powerful psychological advantage over a scale-centric approach.

They go beyond weight loss, encompassing improvements in physical and mental well-being. This broader perspective encourages a healthier lifestyle built on sustainable habits instead of quick fixes or temporary restrictions.

Celebrating your non-scale victories fosters an intrinsic appreciation for healthy choices and behaviors. This shift in motivation makes healthy habits enjoyable and sustainable, leading to long-term results.

Non-scale victories directly link your efforts to immediate, tangible rewards, like increased energy, improved sleep, and your clothes fitting more comfortably. This internal validation sustains motivation beyond the fleeting satisfaction of a lower number on the scale.

When you focus on non-scale victories, you celebrate small, consistent improvements, taking the pressure off achieving specific milestones on a set timeline. This fosters a growth mindset, where small steps and setbacks are seen as opportunities for learning and adaptation, not failures.

Reflecting and appreciating your efforts in healthy eating, exercise, and self-care builds confidence in your ability to make the change. This effectiveness that you have created yourself fuels commitment and consistency in the long run.

Focusing on non-scale victories also acts as a buffer against discouragement when the scale plateaus or fluctuates. By focusing on the positive changes, you prevent negative emotions from derailing your weight-loss adventure.

Your non-scale victories are unique to your individual weight-loss adventure, empowering you to define and celebrate your own definition of success. This fosters a sense of independence and ownership over your weight-loss efforts, increasing your commitment and engagement.

Not only focusing on the scale puts the power in your hands, shifting the emphasis from external factors like the scale to the choices and actions you control. This empowers you to navigate challenges and adapt your approach to achieve permanent results.

Overall, focusing on non-scale victories creates a positive feedback loop fueling motivation, reinforcing healthy habits, and building confidence. It shifts your mindset from a restrictive, number-driven approach to a complete, self-compassionate journey of empowerment and permanent well-being. By celebrating the small wins and focusing on the progress you make every day, you set yourself up for sustainable success beyond the numbers on the scale.

By celebrating non-scale victories, you shift your focus from the fleeting validation of the number on the scale to the true essence of health and well-being. This transformative approach fosters a journey of self-discovery, empowerment, and permanent change. You shed the shackles of number-driven obsessions and embrace the freedom of celebrating progress in all its multifaceted forms.

Try to step away from the scale and turn your attention to the abundance of non-scale victories within you. Celebrate the increased energy, the improved sleep, the mindful food choices, the newfound confidence. In these silent triumphs lies the joy of permanent weight-loss success, composed not of fleeting numbers but of a transformed mind, body, and spirit. Let the celebration begin!

Chapter 18
Relying on Food Rewards vs. Focusing on Intrinsic Rewards

Relying on Food Rewards

Food rewards work by triggering the pleasure centers in our brains, providing a dopamine rush associated with enjoyment. However, our brains adapt to this dopamine boost, requiring increasingly larger or more frequent rewards to achieve the same level of satisfaction. This creates an "indulgent treadmill," where you need more and more food rewards to feel motivated, potentially leading to overeating and sabotaging your weight-loss goals.

Food rewards can activate a phenomenon called "moral licensing," where rewarding yourself with unhealthy food somehow justifies less healthy choices later. The "cheat day" mentality, for example, can lead to overindulging on non-cheat days, negating the progress made during periods of restriction.

Food rewards, by their nature, focus on immediate gratification and the momentary pleasure of a sugary treat or a greasy burger. This overshadows the long-term benefits of healthy eating and sustainable lifestyle changes, lowering your commitment to developing healthy habits.

Frequent food rewards, even small ones, exhaust your willpower and self-control, making it harder to resist temptations in the future. You may find yourself giving in to cravings more easily, chipping away at your commitment to healthy choices.

When you rely on food rewards, your motivation becomes extrinsic, based on the external pleasure of the treat. This weakens your intrinsic motivation for healthy behaviors, which are driven by personal growth and well-being. Over time, the extrinsic reward may lose its potency, leaving you lacking the internal drive to stay on track.

A single slip-up with a food reward can trigger an all-or-nothing mentality, leading to feeling discouraged and abandoning your entire effort. This "one bite leads to the whole cake" thinking can derail your progress and make it harder to get back on track.

By shifting your focus from food rewards to intrinsic well-being, you tap into a powerful source of sustainable motivation that will guide you toward achieving your goals and embracing a healthier, happier you.

Focusing on Intrinsic Rewards

We are conditioned to rely on extrinsic rewards like treats for good behavior or punishment for slip ups. While these can work in the short term, they lack the psychological glue needed for long-term success. Intrinsic rewards, on the other hand, tap into our natural desire for growth, meaning, and self-discovery.

When we celebrate the good choices we make, like whipping up a healthy meal instead of ordering in, we feel empowered and in control. This sense of balance fuels further healthy decisions, creating a positive feedback loop. Every hurdle overcome, every healthy habit solidified, boosts our confidence and self-belief. We witness our own inner strength, building resilience for future challenges.

Celebrating these non-scale victories with support, in person or online, affirms our values and reinforces a sense of belonging. This social validation becomes a strong motivator, reminding us of the "why" behind our efforts.

Celebrating intrinsic rewards sets off a positive chain reaction of increased motivation, sustainable habits, and resilience in the face of setbacks, to name a few.

Each victory, no matter how small, becomes a stepping stone, propelling us forward with intrinsic encouragement instead of fleeting external carrots. The joy of mastering avoidance of the office cake, the pride in choosing a healthy option at a party, these become driving forces in themselves. Do not forget that if you wait around to first feel motivated, it is never going to happen. Action creates motivation, not the other way around. YOU need to start.

As we focus on the joys of movement, the satisfaction of nourishing our bodies, and the improved energy that comes with healthy choices, these habits become intrinsically rewarding. We no longer need external validation to keep going; the internal rewards propel us forward.

Inevitably, there will be bumps on the road. But when our foundation is built on intrinsic rewards, setbacks become opportunities for learning and growth. We see them as detours, not dead ends, and bounce back with renewed resolve, fueled by the internal satisfaction of knowing we are on the right track.

Focusing on intrinsic rewards is not about ignoring the scale altogether. It is about reframing its role. Instead of dictating our happiness, it becomes a data point, one piece of information in the larger tapestry of our progress. We focus on the internal triumphs, the silent victories whispering of a deeper transformation.

This shift in mindset transforms weight loss from a restrictive, uphill battle to a self-discovery adventure. It is about embracing the choices that make us feel strong, energized, and aligned with our values. It is about celebrating the small wins that whisper: "You are doing it. You are on the right path."

So listen to the whispers of intrinsic rewards. They are the fuel for permanent change, the compass guiding us toward a healthier, happier version of ourselves. Celebrate the choices, the progress, the process itself, and watch as the fire within illuminates the path to permanent weight loss and well-being.

Chapter 19
Focusing on the Scale Only vs. Focusing on Health and Energy

Focusing on the Scale Only

Focusing solely on the results on the scale as your primary measure of progress in weight loss can act as a psychological trap, lowering your chances of permanent success.

The scale narrows your focus from a complete view of health and well-being (energy levels, sleep quality, mood) to a single, ever-changing figure. This obsession overshadows the positive changes you are making, leading to discouragement and frustration, even when on the right track.

The scale does not reflect the complex interplay of factors influencing weight, like muscle gain, water retention, hormonal fluctuations, or genetic predispositions. Focusing solely on the number ignores these crucial elements, leading to misinterpretations of progress and unrealistic expectations.

Every dip on the scale can trigger feelings of failure and low self-esteem, while gains may lead to unhealthy celebratory binges. This emotional volatility interferes with long-term consistency and motivation.

The scale can create a negative feedback loop. Discouragement from slow progress or weight plateaus leads to unhealthy coping mechanisms, further hindering your efforts and contributing to a cycle of failure.

Comparing your scale numbers to others, especially through social media, is a recipe for misery. Individual bodies respond differently to weight-loss approaches, and obsessing over comparisons sets you up for frustration and harmful competition.

When the scale becomes the sole arbiter of success, your motivation shifts from intrinsic goals like feeling good and building healthy habits to external validation. This gradually destroys self-belief and makes progress conditional on a number, setting you up for disappointment.

Focusing solely on the scale leads to neglecting your body's hunger and satiety cues. You may overeat or under eat based on the number, ignoring your body's natural wisdom and potentially harming your metabolism.

Obsessing over weight loss disconnects you from the joy of mindful eating and appreciating the nourishment food provides. This leads to restrictive and unsustainable diets, compromising your overall well-being.

In conclusion, the scale, while seemingly objective, offers a limited and potentially deceptive measure of progress in weight loss. Focusing solely on the results has a detrimental impact on your mindset, motivation, and relationship with your body.

Focusing on Health and Energy

The psychology of focusing on health and energy for weight loss taps into powerful motivational forces, increasing your chances of long-term success compared to a scale-centric approach.

Health and energy bring immediate, tangible benefits—better sleep, improved mood, increased stamina. Celebrating these internal rewards encourages intrinsic motivation, driving you forward with a sense of progress and personal growth.

By prioritizing health, you break free from the obsession with achieving a specific weight. This makes the adventure itself enjoyable, filled with small victories and continuous improvement, enhancing long-term consistency.

Healthy habits like mindful eating and regular exercise become the tools for feeling good, not just shrinking a number. This fosters a sustainable approach that integrates seamlessly into your lifestyle.

Prioritizing health puts the power in your hands. You focus on choices you can control—what you eat, how you move, how you rest—instead of obsessing over an external, fluctuating number. This builds self-belief and resilience against setbacks.

Setbacks become opportunities to learn and improve. When your focus is on health, you analyze what drained your energy or disrupted your sleep, adapting your approach with wisdom and self-compassion.

Recognizing and appreciating your efforts reinforces your commitment, even when results are slow or uneven. This fuels perseverance and prevents discouragement when the scale does not budge immediately.

Focusing on health encourages you to appreciate your body for its capabilities and resilience, not just its size. This fosters self-acceptance and positive body image, boosting confidence and motivation.

When health is at the heart of your choices, you move away from guilt and shame associated with weight gain. This creates a kinder, more supportive inner dialogue, propelling you toward positive change without self-punishment.

Setbacks become moments for self-care and understanding, not judgment. This compassionate approach builds a strong foundation for consistent progress, preventing the downward spiral of negativity often triggered by scale numbers.

Focusing on health and energy fosters a positive, proactive psychology for weight loss, shifting motivation from fleeting rewards to intrinsic well-being. This sustainable approach builds resilience, fosters self-acceptance, and empowers you to navigate challenges with self-compassion and unwavering commitment. By prioritizing health, you embark on an adventure of transformation, where weight loss becomes a natural consequence of feeling good in your own skin and embracing a vibrant, healthy lifestyle.

Chapter 20
Giving Up Easily vs. Viewing Setbacks as Temporary

Giving Up Easily

When faced with a setback, be it a missed workout, a sugary treat, or a weight gain, letting go of your aim can feel like giving in to all those challenges. You abandon your healthy routines, return to old habits, and find yourself back at the very beginning, further from your goals than before.

Giving in to temptations and abandoning healthy efforts feels like a harmless indulgence in the moment, but from a psychological perspective, it is a slow erosion of your weight-loss success.

Giving up feeds into a negative self-dialogue. Each slip reinforces thoughts like "I cannot do this" or "it is not worth it," chipping away at your motivation and making long-term commitment seem overwhelming.

Succumbing easily fosters a sense of losing control over your choices. This frustration compounds with each slip, pushing you further away from healthy routines and toward emotional eating or unhealthy coping mechanisms.

Every slip-up, whether a skipped workout or an extra treat, triggers the "all-or-nothing" trap. You think, "I messed up, so why bother?" This mentality leads to abandoning your entire plan, creating a negative feedback loop undermining progress.

Giving up easily can trigger an "all-or-nothing" mentality. A single treat justifies an entire day of indulgence. This mindset gradually destroys consistency and makes the process feel futile.

Giving up easily repeatedly depletes your willpower, making it harder to resist temptations in the future. It is like training your brain to expect and give in to cravings, weakening your resolve and making consistent healthy choices seem increasingly difficult.

Justifying occasional indulgences ("I deserve this after a hard day") activates moral licensing. This creates a false sense of permission to indulge further, blurring the lines between occasional treats and unhealthy overeating.

Every surrender chips away at your self-belief in your ability to achieve your goals. You start doubting your commitment and willpower, fueling feelings of helplessness and making sustained change seem distant.

Giving in easily triggers negative self-talk ("I cannot do this"; "I am a failure"). This internal negativity reinforces the cycle of surrender, creating a self-fulfilling prophecy that hinders your progress.

Each act of giving up, no matter how small, draws from your limited pool of willpower and self-control. This makes subsequent healthy choices feel increasingly difficult, setting you up for a cascade of slip-ups.

Succumbing once creates a justification for future lapses. You tell yourself, "I deserve this after being good all week," eroding the boundaries between healthy and unhealthy behavior and promoting unhealthy choices.

Giving in easily lowers your tolerance for any discomfort associated with healthy habits. A slightly longer workout, a more restrictive meal plan, any challenge triggers the urge to abandon the effort, reducing your ability to adapt and persevere.

When you give up easily, your initial goals and aspirations can feel distant and unattainable. This can lead to a sense of purposelessness, further reducing your motivation and commitment to the process.

Giving in easily in weight loss is not just a single misstep; it is a psychological trap that creates a downward spiral, eroding your willpower, motivation, and connection to your goals. The key to permanent success lies in recognizing the detrimental effects of giving in and developing the resilience and self-compassion to navigate challenges without sacrificing your long-term vision for a healthier you.

Viewing Setbacks as Temporary

Viewing setbacks as temporary bumps on your weight-loss adventure significantly increases your chances of achieving permanent success. It goes beyond simply brushing them off; it is about adopting a resilient mindset that fuels self-compassion, learning opportunities, and unwavering commitment to your goals.

Viewing setbacks as temporary removes the burden of self-blame and promotes the understanding that mistakes and slip-ups are part of the human experience. This self-compassion reduces discouragement and empowers you to move forward without emotional baggage.

Seeing setbacks as temporary learning experiences allows you to identify triggers, analyze missteps, and adjust your approach. This growth mindset prevents future mistakes, strengthens your resilience, and keeps you focused on progress, not perfection.

Temporary setbacks do not define your worth or progress. Recognizing this protects your self-esteem and prevents setbacks from becoming a reflection of your capabilities or identity. You remain empowered to choose healthy behaviors again, one step at a time.

Viewing setbacks as temporary prevents them from shattering your belief in your ability to achieve your goals. This unwavering faith in yourself fuels your motivation and keeps you committed to your long-term vision, even when faced with challenges.

Recognizing setbacks as temporary roadblocks reduces the risk of disengagement and quitting completely. You understand that one slip-up does not erase your progress, empowering you to stay consistent and maintain the healthy habits you have built.

Viewing setbacks as temporary fosters a positive outlook and strengthens your perseverance. You approach challenges with the belief that you can overcome them, building resilience and preventing discouragement from derailing your weight-loss adventure.

Temporary setbacks offer valuable learning opportunities. You can analyze what led to the slip-up, identify triggers, and adjust your strategies to avoid similar situations in the future. This continuous learning refines your approach and sets you up for long-term success.

Learning from setbacks helps you develop healthier coping mechanisms for emotional triggers and challenging situations. These improved habits for managing stress, cravings, or social pressures equip you for future obstacles and prevent emotional eating or impulsive choices.

Recognizing the temporary nature of setbacks encourages flexibility and adaptability. You learn to adjust your approach based on changing circumstances and challenges, ensuring your weight-loss adventure remains sustainable and adaptable to life's inevitable ups and downs.

Viewing setbacks as temporary is not about ignoring them; it is about leveraging them as stepping stones for growth and resilience. It fosters self-compassion, strengthens your commitment, and fuels continuous learning.

Chapter 21
Lack of Resilience vs. Adjust Strategies when Needed

Lack of Resilience

In the pursuit of permanent weight loss, resilience, the psychological muscle that helps you bounce back from challenges, plays a crucial role. A lack of it, however, acts like brittle bones on a demanding trek, increasing your vulnerability to stumble and ultimately sabotaging your weight-loss adventure.

When faced with a challenge, like a missed workout or a weight gain, a lack of resilience narrows your focus. You magnify the setback, catastrophizing its impact and projecting it onto your entire progress, leading to discouragement and despair.

Without the resilience to navigate bumps, you fall prey to the "all-or-nothing" trap. One slip becomes a justification to abandon the entire process, pushing you further away from your goals and reinforcing unhealthy patterns.

Succumbing to setbacks without resilience creates a negative feedback loop. Discouragement leads to decreased motivation, further setbacks follow, and a downward spiral ensues, jeopardizing your long-term commitment.

A lack of resilience makes you susceptible to negative emotions like frustration, anger, and self-blame when faced with challenges. These emotions drain your energy and deplete your motivational reserves, making it harder to maintain healthy habits.

Resilience acts as a buffer against tempting indulgences and unhealthy coping mechanisms. Without it, you are more likely to give in to cravings, abandon healthy routines, and resort to quick fixes that undermine your progress.

As setbacks pile on and resilience dwindles, hope for progress can become a distant dream. Doubt and negativity take hold, leading to a sense of helplessness and a belief that success is unattainable.

Without the resilience to endure discomfort and push through challenges, you might prioritize immediate pleasure over long-term well-being. This compromises your commitment to your goals and makes you susceptible to unhealthy temptations.

A lack of resilience makes it harder to delay gratification or accept that progress takes time and effort. You might chase quick fixes or unsustainable trends, jeopardizing long-term success for fleeting results.

When challenges overwhelm your resilience, your initial commitment to weight loss can waver. The connection to your long-term vision weakens, and the process can feel purposeless, further reducing your motivation to persist.

A lack of resilience acts as a silent saboteur on your weight-loss adventure. It amplifies setbacks, gradually destroys motivation and willpower, and compromises your long-term vision. By understanding the detrimental effects of a fragile mindset, you can prioritize building resilience, equipping yourself with the psychological strength to navigate challenges, bounce back from setbacks, and ultimately achieve permanent success.

Adjust Strategies When Needed

In the ever-changing landscape of weight loss, clinging to rigid strategies is the same as navigating a stormy sea with a fixed sail. Success lies in adaptability, in the willingness to adjust your course when the challenges shift. This psychological flexibility offers powerful advantages on your adventure to permanent weight loss.

Life is dynamic, and rigid weight-loss plans often crumble under the pressures of unexpected events or changing circumstances. Flexibility allows you to adapt your routines to fit your changing needs, making healthy habits easier to sustain in the long run.

No two people respond to weight-loss approaches in the same way. By being flexible, you personalize your weight loss adventure, tuning in to your body's unique cues and tailoring your strategies to your individual needs and preferences.

Being open to feedback is a game-changer. Feedback from others, like a mentor, and from your body. Viewing challenges as opportunities for learning, not failures, allows you to analyze what is working and what is not. You gather data from each experience, both successes and setbacks, to inform and refine your approach.

Flexibility empowers you to experiment with different strategies, dietary choices, and exercise routines. This keeps the weight loss adventure fresh and engaging, fostering a sense of exploration and discovery as you find what works best for you.

Embracing adaptability fosters a growth mindset. You recognize that challenges present opportunities to develop new skills, build resilience, and refine your understanding of your body and its needs.

Rigid adherence to a single strategy can lead to plateaus and discouragement. Flexibility allows you to adjust your approach, tackle obstacles from different angles, and maintain your motivation in the face of temporary setbacks.

Every successful adaptation strengthens your belief in your own ability to overcome challenges and achieve your goals. This self-belief fuels your motivation and keeps you pushing forward, even when the path ahead gets tough.

When you are open to change and experimentation, you prevent weight loss from becoming a monotonous chore. You discover new activities you enjoy, explore different approaches to healthy eating, and keep the weight-loss adventure fresh and engaging.

Rigid adherence to a plan can crumble under the pressure of life's stressors. Flexibility empowers you to navigate challenges like travel, holidays, or emotional stress without abandoning your process or resorting to unhealthy coping mechanisms.

Embracing flexibility is not a sign of weakness but a cornerstone of permanent weight-loss success. By developing a growth mindset, nurturing resilience, and prioritizing sustainable habits, you equip yourself with the psychological agility to navigate the dynamic landscape of health and well-being. When you are willing to adapt, you transform weight loss from a rigid process into a fulfilling adventure of self-discovery, personalized progress, and permanent well-being.

Chapter 22
Using Excuses vs. Taking Accountability

Using Excuses

Excuses can seem like temporary allies, offering justifications for slip-ups and missed opportunities. However, their psychological impact runs deeper, creating a slippery slope that gradually destroys your chances of success and ultimately sets you up for failure.

Excuses shift responsibility for your actions and progress away from you. You blame external factors like time constraints, genetics, or even bad weather, diminishing your sense of ownership and accountability for your health.

Making excuses weakens your initial commitment to change. You rationalize unhealthy choices, chipping away at your resolve and making your goals feel less important and attainable.

Excuses create a disconnect between your stated values and your actual actions. You might value health and well-being, but justifying unhealthy choices through excuses compromises your integrity and gradually destroys your motivation.

Excuses provide permission for unhealthy indulgences and missed workouts. You convince yourself of their validity, creating a pattern of justification that can snowball into a cycle of unhealthy choices.

Making excuses often leads to self-blame and negativity. You internalize these justifications as personal shortcomings, reinforcing a downward spiral of self-doubt and undermining your belief in your own ability to succeed.

Excuses act as a psychological barrier, diverting your focus from taking concrete steps toward your goals. You become preoccupied with rationalizing your inaction, neglecting the essential task of planning and implementing healthy habits.

Excuses prevent you from learning from challenges and setbacks. You dismiss them as external obstacles, missing valuable opportunities to analyze your choices and adjust your approach for future success.

When you cling to excuses, you avoid confronting the limitations of your current approach. This reduces your ability to experiment, adapt, and refine your strategies for maximum effectiveness.

Excuses often become a comfortable crutch, preventing you from pushing yourself outside your comfort zone and taking on new challenges. This stagnation reduces progress and keeps you stuck in a cycle of ineffective routines.

Making excuses, while seemingly harmless, poses a significant threat to your weight-loss adventure. They compromise your commitment and accountability, enable unhealthy habits, and hinder learning and growth. By recognizing their deceptive nature and prioritizing accountability, you can break free from the cycle of excuses and empower yourself to build a foundation of permanent change.

Taking Accountability

Taking accountability is not about tracking calories or checking off workout boxes. It is a powerful psychological shift that rewires your mindset, fuels motivation, and increases your chances of reaching your goals.

When you take accountability, you acknowledge your role in your progress. This strengthens your belief in your own ability to make positive changes and achieve your goals, fueling your motivation and perseverance.

Accountability moves you from a passive recipient of circumstances to an active driver of your health. This ownership empowers you to make choices, adjust strategies, and navigate challenges with a sense of purpose and control.

Owning your weight-loss adventure strengthens your commitment to change. You become invested in your progress, not just compliant with external dictates, leading to a deeper and more sustainable engagement with your goals.

Accountability encourages active monitoring of your choices and their impact on your well-being. This promotes introspection, helping you identify patterns and triggers and make informed decisions for future progress.

Taking accountability fosters a willingness to analyze setbacks and challenges objectively. You approach them as opportunities for learning and growth, rather than reasons for self-blame or discouragement.

Owning your process encourages experimentation and a flexible approach. You embrace feedback, make adjustments based on your own experiences, and continuously refine your strategies for optimal results.

Accountability allows you to celebrate successes as a testament to your efforts, strengthening your self-esteem and confidence. This positive reinforcement encourages further motivation and strengthens your resilience against setbacks.

Owning your weight-loss adventure prevents you from getting entangled in the blame game. You avoid externalizing responsibility or resorting to self-criticism, fostering a growth mindset and focusing on solutions over excuses.

Accountability provides a sense of personal satisfaction and fulfillment when you stay on track, even during challenges. This intrinsic reward system keeps you motivated, especially when external support or rewards might dwindle.

Taking accountability is a cornerstone of permanent weight-loss success. It cultivates ownership, enhances self-awareness, and builds resilience. When you embrace responsibility for your weight-loss adventure, you transform challenges into opportunities for learning and growth, propelling yourself toward sustainable habits and a healthier, happier you. Remember, it is your adventure, and taking ownership empowers you to navigate it with purpose, resilience, and ultimately, achieve permanent success.

Chapter 23

Closing the Gap: From Awareness to Action

Congratulations! By uncovering your personal "passengers" influencing your weight-loss adventure, you have taken a crucial step toward permanent success. Now comes the empowering part: bridging the gap between who you are and who you want to be. Through reflecting on your own behavior and understanding what you do and think during weight-loss efforts, you will identify the behaviors to nurture and those to leave behind, paving the way for sustainable change.

Imagine your current weight-loss efforts as a puzzle. You have identified some key pieces—your behaviors. Now, compare them to the puzzle picture representing your desired outcome. Do the pieces fit seamlessly, creating a complete and vibrant image? Or are there gaps, missing pieces representing behaviors that reduce your progress?

Permanent change is more of an adventure of ups and downs to get to your destination. There will be bumps along the road, moments when old passengers try to sneak back in. But with awareness, self-compassion, and a commitment to continuous improvement, you can bridge the gap between your current reality and your desired weight-loss vision.

Embrace the power of mindful personal reflection and action. Keep refining your puzzle, replacing problem pieces with empowering ones. Move forward, empowered and equipped, and claim your permanent success!

www.ingramcontent.com/pod-product-compliance
Lightning Source LLC
Chambersburg PA
CBHW040823300326
41914CB00063B/1483